God's
STORY

{AS TOLD BY JOHN}

W0010950

God's
STORY

{AS TOLD BY JOHN}

ESV

ENGLISH STANDARD VERSION

CROSSWAY BOOKS
A PUBLISHING MINISTRY OF GOOD NEWS PUBLISHERS
WHEATON, ILLINOIS

God's Story: As Told by John
Copyright © 2006 by Youth for Christ/USA

Contributing Writers: Greg Boyer, Trent Bushnell, Jack Crabtree,
Nina Edwards, Jenny Morgan and Don Talley.

The 3Story® concept and all 3Story® material © 2006 by Youth for
Christ/USA®.

Published in association with the literary agency of Wolgemuth and
Associates, Inc.

The Bible text of the Gospel of John is from The Holy Bible, English
Standard Version®. Copyright © 2001 by Crossway Bibles, a
publishing ministry of Good News Publishers. All rights reserved.

Cover and Interior Design: Josh Dennis

Library of Congress Catalog Card number 2006008128

Printed in the United States of America
06 07 08 09 DP 5 4 3 2 1

>>CONTENTS

My Life, My Story viii

3Story Overview: God's Story, My Story,
    Their Story x

Ten 3Story Principles for Faith-Sharing xiv

3Story Prayer Wish List xviii

The Gospel of John, with 3Story Scenes 1

What Is "Abiding"? 68-69

Definitions of 3Story Words and Phrases 91

Verse Memorization Index...................................94

Prayer: Getting Started in a Lifelong
    Relationship with Jesus Christ......................97

MY LIFE, MY STORY

Hi. I'm Mary, I'm seventeen, and I'm a Christian. At times the details of my life—My Story—seem really complicated. Questions fill my mind, temptations capture my heart, and sometimes I feel uncertain and really unsure of myself. Until I understood what living an authentic Christian life was all about, I lived a boring, sometimes hypocritical Christian life. When I started reading God's Story through the eyes of Jesus' best friend, John, a huge, bright lightbulb went off above my head. My Story took on so much more life and meaning. Don't get me wrong—I don't have it all together, but I am learning.

Once I started to let My Story connect with more of God's Story, I began to see some of the tie points between Jesus and me. Then I started seeing the ways that my friends' stories—Their Story—also intersected with God's Story.

I am really glad Jesus came to earth for me. I want to hear His voice. Once I understood how to listen to God better, I began to listen better to my friends, too. Soon, it all began to happen naturally. I began to experience a whole new way of living. (It's so much easier to tell my friends how much I need Jesus, than to try to convince them that they need Jesus.) I stopped feeling scared, and I rarely feel defensive; there's nothing to defend! God's Story is amazing and it includes everyone, even people who don't yet want to be included. God is patient. He has everything covered. I just get to tell My Story, while working harder to listen to Their Story. I get to help my friends see how God wants to have this amazing relationship with them. I get to explain how much I need God every day of my life!

Anyway—try it. It's working for me. Read God's Story from John's perspective. Ask God's Holy Spirit to help you. Go slowly; He's in no hurry. He has all the time in the universe to love you. You can be real. You can learn to trust Him. You can learn to be the good news while you learn to speak good news. It's all about connecting three amazing, heroic stories: God's Story, My Story, and Their Story.

GOD'S STORY, MY STORY, THEIR STORY

At its heart, 3Story is a way of living. It's a way of understanding the process of change you experience in your relationship with God and with other people. Within a relationship with Jesus Christ and a relationship with another person, sharing your faith happens naturally. It's one life touching another life: "life-on-life" ministry.

NO RULES, NO FORMULAS, JUST RELATIONSHIPS

Think of three circles representing three stories—**God's Story**, **My Story**, and **Their Story** (see illustration, p. xii). The more the three circles overlap, the more a person can experience and see the power of the gospel of Jesus Christ.

Jesus is already close to your friends who might not know Him. When you draw close to people, you allow your story to overlap with Their Story. Granted, your friends may not yet realize that God is initiating a relationship with them. But you have the amazing privilege of helping your friends become aware of God and His work in their lives.

The three circles represent the content of the stories of three

What Is 3Story All About?

>> **3Story** is always about abiding in Christ, loving and listening to Him continuously, depending on Him, taking our very life breath from Him, living through Him with the help of His Holy Spirit.

>> **3Story** begins with a rich understanding of the content of the three stories, with a crucial focus on the most important story of all, God's Story.

>> **3Story** connects people and stories—me, my friends, and God. The more the stories and lives connect, the more powerful the impact of the gospel can be.

>> **3Story** Evangelism is not new; it is a return to a way of living that characterized Jesus' life and the lives of His disciples.

lives. Within these three stories, something can be revealed or learned about three people and three relationships. You can learn how to make important relational connections, which will enable you to live an authentic Christian life.

3Story Diagram

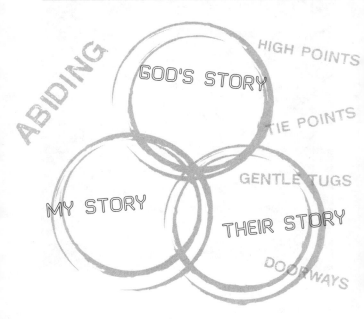

DISCOVER THEIR STORY THROUGH LOVING AND LISTENING.

DISCLOSE MY STORY BY BEING REAL AND TALKING ABOUT JESUS.

Jump into God's Story right now! Let John, one of Jesus' best friends, help you learn something new about Jesus Christ. The Holy Spirit invites you to engage in an incredible adventure of discovering how thrilling God's Story can be for you and for your friends. While reading the Gospel of John, you will observe the ways Jesus experienced relationships with people:

How Did Jesus Relate?

>> **Jesus connected with people** and He listened.

>> **Jesus loved people** where they were.

>> **Jesus tailored the sharing of God's Story** to the individual.

>> **Jesus was never distracted** when He met with people.

>> **Jesus asked questions** to draw people out.

>> **Jesus' message was always consistent** but never generic.

>> **Jesus was personal, honest, and compassionate.**

God is inviting you and your friends to do more than simply understand God's Story. He wants you to surrender to His story. He wants each of us to give ourselves over to Him daily, moment by moment, integrating our entire lives—all of My Story—into God's Story. That's really living!

TEN 3STORY PRINCIPLES FOR FAITH-SHARING

SECOND CORINTHIANS 5:14-21 IS THE FOUNDATIONAL PASSAGE FOR 3STORY LIVING.

> For the love of Christ controls us, because we have concluded this: that one has died for all, therefore all have died; and he died for all, that those who live might no longer live for themselves but for him who for their sake died and was raised. From now on, therefore, we regard no one according to the flesh. Even though we once regarded Christ according to the flesh, we regard him thus no longer. Therefore, if anyone is in Christ, he is a new creation. The old has passed away; behold, the new has come. All this is from God, who through Christ reconciled us to himself and gave us the ministry of reconciliation; that is, in

Christ God was reconciling the world to himself, not counting their trespasses against them, and entrusting to us the message of reconciliation. Therefore, we are ambassadors for Christ, God making his appeal through us. We implore you on behalf of Christ, be reconciled to God. For our sake he made him to be sin who knew no sin, so that in him we might become the righteousness of God.

1. **It's stories more than steps.** (Acts 17:27-28)

   >> 3Story is about bringing three stories together in a natural way. It is not taking people through a sequence of predetermined steps.

2. **It's honesty more than perfection.** (Philippians 3:9b, 12-14)

   >> 3Story asks us to be honest, not perfect.

3. **It's them more than you.** (1 Thessalonians 2:8)

   >> 3Story allows our friends to be who they are as we discover Their Story.

4. **It's questions more than answers.** (John 4:1-30)

>> 3Story is more about asking questions than giving answers. Christians often offer answers to questions that "not-yet-followers" of Christ aren't even asking.

5. **It's listening more than telling.** (Colossians 4:6)

>> 3Story starts out with listening, not preaching. It's built on the assumption that people listen to people who listen.

6. **It's hope more than judgment.** (1 Peter 3:15-16a)

>> 3Story is primarily about sharing our own need for Jesus and our hope in Him rather than judging other people's lifestyles, words, or choices.

7. **It's the Holy Spirit more than program.** (Romans 8:26-30)

>> 3Story means being led by God's Spirit in our relationships. It's not working through tips or techniques to maneuver God into a conversation. It's about bringing Jesus' Story into a relationship at just the right moment.

8. **It's circular more than linear.** (John 4:1-30)

>> 3Story invites people to discover parts of Jesus' Story that are most relevant to them at that moment.

Jesus' Story doesn't come to everybody in the same order or with the same words.

9. It's love more than knowledge.
(1 Corinthians 13:1-2, 13)

>> 3Story believes in the biblical view of the power of love. In the world in which we live, love wins people's hearts.

10. It's contributing more than controlling.
(1 Peter 3:16a)

>> 3Story is not about controlling. Rather, it's about allowing conversations to flow freely and bringing Jesus' Story naturally into discussions.

Make a "wish list" of all the people you know whom you hope will have a relationship with Jesus Christ. Write their names on the following page. Begin now to pray daily for the people on your wish list. (There is a suggested prayer below that you can use to start.) With the guidance of God's Holy Spirit, begin today to listen to Their Stories and love them well.

Here are questions to help you gather the names of the people you love onto your wish list:

>> **Who do you wish had a relationship with Jesus?**

>> **Whom in your life do you want to connect with God's Story?**

>> **Whom do you have a spiritual concern for right now?**

Be sure to have at least one classmate, one family member, and one close friend on your list. How you treat people who are outside of your specific group or church is an important measurement of your spiritual health. So you want to have lots of different people on your wish list.

Ask God to bring people into your life whom He can love through you. As an expression of your faith that Jesus is at work in your life, add an extra number or two at the bottom of your wish list for new friends that God wants you to meet. He is already working in their lives and He wants to use you to love them. Be open to His Spirit working in you.

MY WISH LIST

1. _____

2. _____

3. _____

4. _____

5. _____

A PRAYER

Dear Lord,

Help me to love these people well. Help me to really listen to them when opportunities arise, and not just listen to their words, but to their hearts! Help me never to treat them as projects, but help me to really love them, like You do. Help them to see how much You love them.

Please guide me as I read Your Story through the eyes of Your friend, John. Will You speak clearly to me? Will You gently correct me when I need correction? Please comfort me when I go astray, and lead me when I fall off the path You intend for me. And, Jesus, help me to recognize Your love for me and for my friends. I want to be surprised by Your goodness. I want to trust You more every day. I want to love You more than anything else in the world.

Thank You for living Your life for me. Help me to live my life and My Story for You. Thank You for dying on the cross for me. Thank You for rising from the dead for me. Thank You that You are alive today. I need You, and I feel so very grateful for You. Amen.

The Word Became Flesh

1 In the beginning was the Word, and the Word was with God, and the Word was God. **²**He was in the beginning with God. **³**All things were made through him, and without him was not any thing made that was made. **⁴**In him was life,[1] and the life was the light of men. **⁵**The light shines in the darkness, and the darkness has not overcome it.

⁶There was a man sent from God, whose name was John. **⁷**He came as a witness, to bear witness about the light, that all might believe through him. **⁸**He was not the light, but came to bear witness about the light.

⁹The true light, which enlightens everyone, was coming into the world. **¹⁰**He was in the world, and the world was made through him, yet the world did not know him. **¹¹**He came to his own,[2] and his own people[3] did not receive him. **¹²**But to all who did receive him, who believed in his name, he gave the right to become children of God, **¹³**who were born, not of blood nor of the will of the flesh nor of the will of man, but of God.

¹⁴And the Word became flesh and dwelt among us, and we have seen his glory, glory as of the only Son from the Father, full of grace and truth. **¹⁵**(John bore witness about him, and cried out, "This was he of whom I said, 'He who comes after me ranks before me, because he was before me.'") **¹⁶**And from his fullness we have all received, grace upon grace. **¹⁷**For the law was given through Moses; grace and

---

1 Or *was not any thing made. That which has been made was life in him*   2 Greek *to his own things*; that is, to his own domain, or to his own people   3 *People* is implied in Greek

truth came through Jesus Christ. [18] No one has ever seen God; the only God,[1] who is at the Father's side,[2] he has made him known.

The Testimony of John the Baptist

[19] And this is the testimony of John, when the Jews sent priests and Levites from Jerusalem to ask him, "Who are you?" [20] He confessed, and did not deny, but confessed, "I am not the Christ." [21] And they asked him, "What then? Are you Elijah?" He said, "I am not." "Are you the Prophet?" And he answered, "No." [22] So they said to him, "Who are you? We need to give an answer to those who sent us. What do you say about yourself?" [23] He said, "I am *a* the voice of one crying out in the wilderness, 'Make straight[3] the way of the Lord,' as the prophet Isaiah said."

[24] (Now they had been sent from the Pharisees.) [25] They asked him, "Then why are you baptizing, if you are neither the Christ, nor Elijah, nor the Prophet?" [26] John answered them, "I baptize with water, but among you stands one you do not know, [27] even he who comes after me, the strap of whose sandal I am not worthy to untie." [28] These things took place in Bethany across the Jordan, where John was baptizing.

Behold, the Lamb of God

[29] The next day he saw Jesus coming toward him, and said, "Behold, the Lamb of God, who takes away the sin of the world! [30] This is

---

[1] Or *the only One, who is God*; some manuscripts *the only Son* [2] Greek *in the bosom of the Father* [3] Or *crying out, 'In the wilderness make straight* [a] Isa. 40:3

he of whom I said, 'After me comes a man who ranks before me, because he was before me.' ³¹ I myself did not know him, but for this purpose I came baptizing with water, that he might be revealed to Israel." ³² And John bore witness: "I saw the Spirit descend from heaven like a dove, and it remained on him. ³³ I myself did not know him, but he who sent me to baptize with water said to me, 'He on whom you see the Spirit descend and remain, this is he who baptizes with the Holy Spirit.' ³⁴ And I have seen and have borne witness that this is the Son of God."

Jesus Calls the First Disciples

³⁵ The next day again John was standing with two of his disciples, ³⁶ and he looked at Jesus as he walked by and said, "Behold, the Lamb of God!" ³⁷ The two disciples heard him say this, and they followed Jesus. ³⁸ Jesus turned and saw them following and said to them, "What are you seeking?" And they said to him, "Rabbi" (which means Teacher), "where are you staying?" ³⁹ He said to them, "Come and you will see." So they came and saw where he was staying, and they stayed with him that day, for it was about the tenth hour.[1] ⁴⁰ One of the two who heard John speak and followed Jesus[2] was Andrew, Simon Peter's brother. ⁴¹ He first found his own brother Simon and said to him, "We have found the Messiah" (which means Christ). ⁴² He brought him to Jesus. Jesus looked at him and said, "So you are Simon the son of John? You shall be called Cephas" (which means Peter[3]).

---

1 That is, about 4 P.M.   2 Greek *him*   3 *Cephas* and *Peter* are from the word for *rock* in Aramaic and Greek, respectively

Jesus Calls Philip and Nathanael

⁴³ The next day Jesus decided to go to Galilee. He found Philip and said to him, "Follow me." ⁴⁴ Now Philip was from Bethsaida, the city of Andrew and Peter. ⁴⁵ Philip found Nathanael and said to him, "We have found him of whom Moses in the Law and also the prophets wrote, Jesus of Nazareth, the son of Joseph." ⁴⁶ Nathanael said to him, "Can anything good come out of Nazareth?" Philip said to him, "Come and see." ⁴⁷ Jesus saw Nathanael coming toward him and said of him, "Behold, an Israelite indeed, in whom there is no deceit!" ⁴⁸ Nathanael said to him, "How do you know me?" Jesus answered him, "Before Philip called you, when you were under the fig tree, I saw you." ⁴⁹ Nathanael answered him, "Rabbi, you are the Son of God! You are the King of Israel!" ⁵⁰ Jesus answered him, "Because I said to you, 'I saw you under the fig tree,' do you believe? You will see greater things than these." ⁵¹ And he said to him, "Truly, truly, I say to you, you will see heaven opened, and the angels of God ascending and descending on the Son of Man."

The Wedding at Cana

2 On the third day there was a wedding at Cana in Galilee, and the mother of Jesus was there. ² Jesus also was invited to the wedding with his disciples. ³ When the wine ran out, the mother of Jesus said to him, "They have no wine." ⁴ And Jesus

said to her, "Woman, what does this have to do with me? My hour has not yet come." [5] His mother said to the servants, "Do whatever he tells you."

[6] Now there were six stone water jars there for the Jewish rites of purification, each holding twenty or thirty gallons. [1] [7] Jesus said to the servants, "Fill the jars with water." And they filled them up to the brim. [8] And he said to them, "Now draw some out and take it to the master of the feast." So they took it. [9] When the master of the feast tasted the water now become wine, and did not know where it came from (though the servants who had drawn the water knew), the master of the feast called the bridegroom [10] and said to him, "Everyone serves the good wine first, and when people have drunk freely, then the poor wine. But you have kept the good wine until now." [11] This, the first of his signs, Jesus did at Cana in Galilee, and manifested his glory. And his disciples believed in him.

[12] After this he went down to Capernaum, with his mother and his brothers [2] and his disciples, and they stayed there for a few days.

Jesus Cleanses the Temple

[13] The Passover of the Jews was at hand, and Jesus went up to Jerusalem. [14] In the temple he found those who were selling oxen and sheep and pigeons, and the money-changers sitting there. [15] And making a whip of cords, he drove them all out of the temple, with the sheep and oxen. And he poured out the coins of the money-changers and overturned their tables. [16] And he told those who sold the

1 Greek *two or three measures* (*metrētas*); a *metrētēs* was about 10 gallons or 35 liters 2 Or *brothers and sisters.* The plural Greek word *adelphoi* (translated "brothers") refers to siblings in a family. In New Testament usage, depending on the context, *adelphoi* may refer either to *brothers* or to *brothers and sisters*

Jesus Calls Philip and Nathanael

>>COME AND SEE!

Have you ever found something so cool—so great—that you immediately called up your friends and said, "Get over here. You gotta see this!"? That's what Philip did when he found Jesus. He ran to his friend Nathanael and said, "Come and see."

Jesus still seeks disciples today. Jesus is calling you to be His disciple. What will happen if you really give your life to Him? Where will He take you?

When Jesus calls, do you run to Him or do you run away from Him? You can run and try to hide—from yourself, from life, from people, from Jesus. You can hide in:

>> loud-music-all-the-time places

>> drunken places

>> materialistic places

>> sexual places

>> leave-me-alone places

You can even hide inside religion! (Think about that one.)

When Jesus finds Philip and Nathanael, they don't run from Him. They don't hide. So Jesus builds deep relationships with them, becoming their Savior, their mentor, and their friend. Jesus becomes their Champion, their Lord for the rest of their lives. He shows them mighty miracles. He opens their eyes so they see heaven. They begin living eternal life now.

Jesus wants the same for you. He's seeking you; He wants you to be His disciple. Will you accept His invitation and His calling? Will you hook your story into Jesus' eternal story?

Jesus finds His disciples, and they find their friends! It's a pattern. When Jesus finds Andrew, Andrew finds Peter. When Jesus finds Philip, Philip finds Nathanael and says, "Come and see!" When Jesus finds you, you'll want to find your friends.

As you begin following Jesus, you will want to gently pursue others with God's Story. This will come naturally because God will be working in you, helping you honestly love and care for others. You will want to really know them. Your story will overlap with Their Story. You will abide with Jesus, and you will connect with your friends. They will meet Jesus in you. This will be sweet.

Allow Jesus to find you, love you, and forgive you. Live a 3Story life—to God's praise and glory!

>> Don't hide from Jesus.

>> Connect God's Story to your story.

>> Let your heart go out to your friends.

>> Pray that Jesus will work His miracles in your heart and in your life.

>> Tell your friends to "come and see" what Jesus has done for you—and what He wants to do for them.

pigeons, "Take these things away; do not make my Father's house a house of trade." **17** His disciples remembered that it was written, *a* "Zeal for your house will consume me."

18 So the Jews said to him, "What sign do you show us for doing these things?" **19** Jesus answered them, "Destroy this temple, and in three days I will raise it up." **20** The Jews then said, "It has taken forty-six years to build this temple, and will you raise it up in three days?" **21** But he was speaking about the temple of his body. **22** When therefore he was raised from the dead, his disciples remembered that he had said this, and they believed the Scripture and the word that Jesus had spoken.

Jesus Knows What Is in Man

23 Now when he was in Jerusalem at the Passover Feast, many believed in his name when they saw the signs that he was doing. **24** But Jesus on his part did not entrust himself to them, because he knew all people **25** and needed no one to bear witness about man, for he himself knew what was in man.

You Must Be Born Again

3 Now there was a man of the Pharisees named Nicodemus, a ruler of the Jews. **2** This man came to Jesus[1] by night and said to him, "Rabbi, we know that you are a teacher come from God, for no one can do these signs that you do unless God is with him."

1 Greek *him*   a Ps. 69:9

³Jesus answered him, "Truly, truly, I say to you, unless one is born again[1] he cannot see the kingdom of God." ⁴Nicodemus said to him, "How can a man be born when he is old? Can he enter a second time into his mother's womb and be born?" ⁵Jesus answered, "Truly, truly, I say to you, unless one is born of water and the Spirit, he cannot enter the kingdom of God. ⁶That which is born of the flesh is flesh, and that which is born of the Spirit is spirit.[2] ⁷Do not marvel that I said to you, 'You must be born again.' ⁸The wind[3] blows where it wishes, and you hear its sound, but you do not know where it comes from or where it goes. So it is with everyone who is born of the Spirit."

⁹Nicodemus said to him, "How can these things be?" ¹⁰Jesus answered him, "Are you the teacher of Israel and yet you do not understand these things? ¹¹Truly, truly, I say to you, we speak of what we know, and bear witness to what we have seen, but you do not receive our testimony. ¹²If I have told you earthly things and you do not believe, how can you believe if I tell you heavenly things? ¹³No one has ascended into heaven except he who descended from heaven, the Son of Man.[4] ¹⁴And as Moses lifted up the serpent in the wilderness, so must the Son of Man be lifted up, ¹⁵that whoever believes in him may have eternal life.[5]

For God So Loved the World

¹⁶"For God so loved the world,[6] that he gave his only Son, that whoever believes in him should not perish but have eternal life.

---

1 Or *from above*; the Greek is purposely ambiguous and can mean both *again* and *from above*; also verse 7   2 The same Greek word means both *wind* and *spirit*   3 The same Greek word means both *wind* and *spirit*   4 Some manuscripts add *who is in heaven*   5 Some interpreters hold that the quotation ends at verse 15   6 Or *For this is how God loved the world*

17 For God did not send his Son into the world to condemn the world, but in order that the world might be saved through him. 18 Whoever believes in him is not condemned, but whoever does not believe is condemned already, because he has not believed in the name of the only Son of God. 19 And this is the judgment: the light has come into the world, and people loved the darkness rather than the light because their deeds were evil. 20 For everyone who does wicked things hates the light and does not come to the light, lest his deeds should be exposed. 21 But whoever does what is true comes to the light, so that it may be clearly seen that his deeds have been carried out in God."

John the Baptist Exalts Christ

22 After this Jesus and his disciples went into the Judean country-side, and he remained there with them and was baptizing. 23 John also was baptizing at Aenon near Salim, because water was plentiful there, and people were coming and being baptized 24 (for John had not yet been put in prison).

25 Now a discussion arose between some of John's disciples and a Jew over purification. 26 And they came to John and said to him, "Rabbi, he who was with you across the Jordan, to whom you bore witness—look, he is baptizing, and all are going to him." 27 John answered, "A person cannot receive even one thing unless it is given him from heaven. 28 You yourselves bear me witness, that I said, 'I am not the Christ, but I have been sent before him.' 29 The one who

has the bride is the bridegroom. The friend of the bridegroom, who stands and hears him, rejoices greatly at the bridegroom's voice. Therefore this joy of mine is now complete. ³⁰ He must increase, but I must decrease."[1]

³¹ He who comes from above is above all. He who is of the earth belongs to the earth and speaks in an earthly way. He who comes from heaven is above all. ³² He bears witness to what he has seen and heard, yet no one receives his testimony. ³³ Whoever receives his testimony sets his seal to this, that God is true. ³⁴ For he whom God has sent utters the words of God, for he gives the Spirit without measure. ³⁵ The Father loves the Son and has given all things into his hand. ³⁶ Whoever believes in the Son has eternal life; whoever does not obey the Son shall not see life, but the wrath of God remains on him.

Jesus and the Woman of Samaria

4 Now when Jesus learned that the Pharisees had heard that Jesus was making and baptizing more disciples than John ² (although Jesus himself did not baptize, but only his disciples), ³ he left Judea and departed again for Galilee. ⁴ And he had to pass through Samaria. ⁵ So he came to a town of Samaria called Sychar, near the field that Jacob had given to his son Joseph. ⁶ Jacob's well was there; so Jesus, wearied as he was from his journey, was sitting beside the well. It was about the sixth hour.[2]

⁷ There came a woman of Samaria to draw water. Jesus said to her,

---

1 Some interpreters hold that the quotation continues through verse 36 2 That is, about noon

Jesus and Nicodemus

>>STARING AT THE CEILING

Mike had it all together . . . mostly. A seventeen-year-old Christian and a leader in his youth group, he knew how to act and what music to listen to. He had memorized a few Bible verses. He knew how things were supposed to run in church. Deep inside, however, Mike felt unfulfilled. Everything he did, even the good things, left him feeling empty.

Nicodemus must have felt the same dissatisfaction. Why else would he take such a huge risk to meet with Jesus? Nicodemus was a Pharisee. In general, the Pharisees hated Jesus. Jesus was a threat to their nicely packaged religion. He challenged their control, arrogance, and hypocrisy. More interested in writing new laws than in getting to know God, Pharisees were the religious rule-makers of their time.

Jesus made them nervous.

Nicodemus had power, respect, and the right religious answers; yet he was not satisfied. Nicodemus wanted something more. The night he talked to Jesus, Nicodemus placed a lot on the line. His reputation would have been ruined if anyone had seen them together. But his hunger for truth was stronger than his fear. Curious about Jesus, Nicodemus went and listened, perhaps for the first time, to Jesus' voice.

Mike looked a lot like a Pharisee, too. He had religious knowledge—he knew *about* Jesus—but he didn't *know* Jesus. He didn't listen to Jesus and didn't really want to change. During a particularly discouraging time, Mike was restless and feeling overwhelmed by emptiness.

One night, staring at the ceiling, Mike felt compelled to listen to Jesus. He seemed to "hear" Jesus speaking to him in his heart and mind. Jesus told him that knowledge about Him wasn't enough. Mike needed a real, true *relationship* with Jesus, not another religious experience. Mike could no longer be satisfied with the facts about God's Story. He knew he had to allow his story to intersect with God's Story in a fresh way. More importantly, Jesus wanted to help Mike change. Mike began to shift from being a religious person to a courageous follower of Jesus Christ.

Nicodemus had to face the truth about himself, too. Any change, especially deep soul-change, is difficult. Jesus said, "You must be born again." That means allowing God's Story to intersect with My Story so that He can rearrange attitudes, behaviors, desires, dreams—everything. Being born again is like starting over, getting a second chance, and living life close to Jesus. Jesus offers new life to everyone.

Mike was born again that night while staring at the ceiling and listening to Jesus. In the end, Nicodemus also became very close to Jesus; so close, in fact, that he was one of two men who took Jesus' body off that brutal cross after He died (see John 19:38-42). They buried Jesus' body, not yet knowing that He was about to rise from the dead for them, for Mike, for all of us.

>> Thank Jesus that He died for you.

>> Thank Jesus for rising from the dead for you.

>> Thank Jesus that He died and rose from the dead for your friends.

>> Ask Jesus to help you surrender your life, every day, to Him.

>> Ask Jesus to help you tell His story.

Perhaps you are as courageous as Nicodemus. Perhaps you are dissatisfied with your religion. Are you willing to let Jesus change you?

Stare at the ceiling tonight. Ask God to talk to you. Then listen.

"Give me a drink." 8(For his disciples had gone away into the city to buy food.) 9The Samaritan woman said to him, "How is it that you, a Jew, ask for a drink from me, a woman of Samaria?" (For Jews have no dealings with Samaritans.) 10Jesus answered her, "If you knew the gift of God, and who it is that is saying to you, 'Give me a drink,' you would have asked him, and he would have given you living water." 11The woman said to him, "Sir, you have nothing to draw water with, and the well is deep. Where do you get that living water? 12Are you greater than our father Jacob? He gave us the well and drank from it himself, as did his sons and his livestock." 13Jesus said to her, "Everyone who drinks of this water will be thirsty again, 14but whoever drinks of the water that I will give him will never be thirsty forever. The water that I will give him will become in him a spring of water welling up to eternal life." 15The woman said to him, "Sir, give me this water, so that I will not be thirsty or have to come here to draw water."

16Jesus said to her, "Go, call your husband, and come here." 17The woman answered him, "I have no husband." Jesus said to her, "You are right in saying, 'I have no husband'; 18for you have had five husbands, and the one you now have is not your husband. What you have said is true." 19The woman said to him, "Sir, I perceive that you are a prophet. 20Our fathers worshiped on this mountain, but you say that in Jerusalem is the place where people ought to worship." 21Jesus said to her, "Woman, believe me, the hour is coming when neither on this mountain nor in Jerusalem will you worship the Father. 22You worship what you do not know; we worship what we know, for salvation is from the Jews. 23But the hour is coming, and is now here, when the true worshipers will worship the Father in spirit and truth, for the Father is seeking such people to worship him. [24]God is spirit, and those who worship him must worship in spirit and truth." [25]The woman said to him, "I know that Messiah is coming (he who is called Christ). When he comes, he will tell us all things." [26]Jesus said to her, "I who speak to you am he."

[27]Just then his disciples came back. They marveled that he was talking with a woman, but no one said, "What do you seek?" or, "Why are you talking with her?" [28]So the woman left her water jar and went away into town and said to the people, [29]"Come, see a man who told me all that I ever did. Can this be the Christ?" [30]They went out of the town and were coming to him.

[31]Meanwhile the disciples were urging him, saying, "Rabbi, eat." [32]But he said to them, "I have food to eat that you do not know about." [33]So the disciples said to one another, "Has anyone brought him something to eat?" [34]Jesus said to them, "My food is to do the will of him who sent me and to accomplish his work. [35]Do you not say, 'There are yet four months, then comes the harvest'? Look, I tell you, lift up your eyes, and see that the fields are white for harvest. [36]Already the one who reaps is receiving wages and gathering fruit for eternal life, so that sower and reaper may rejoice together. [37]For here the saying holds true, 'One sows and another reaps.' [38]I sent you to reap that for which you did not labor. Others have labored, and you have entered into their labor."

[39]Many Samaritans from that town believed in him because of the woman's testimony, "He told me all that I ever did." [40]So when

The Woman at the Well

>>UNCONDITIONAL LOVE

Jesus' story collides with the Samaritan woman's story when she least expects it.

>> He is a mystery; she is curious.
>> He is all-knowing; she doesn't know herself.
>> He is loving; she feels unlovable.

When we see the pieces of God's Story connect with our own, sometimes it is in small, almost unnoticeable ways. Sometimes, as in the story of the woman at the well, God's Story connects with ours with immediate power.

"Please give me a drink." With that one phrase Jesus enters this woman's world. Does he need a drink? Maybe, but more importantly the water is the tie point, the connection between her story and God's Story. He knows her doorway—her specific need—is unconditional love. Jesus' request for water creates the opportunity to connect God's Story to her story.

Cautiously the woman reveals a bit of her story to Him. She confesses that she doesn't have a husband. Mysteriously, Jesus already knows all about her. He confirms that He knows she has been living a disgraceful life. And, without words, He also reveals His unconditional love for her.

A miracle occurs. Lots of the townspeople know of this woman and her lifestyle, but no one loves her in spite of it. God's Story of unconditional love has suddenly become her story, and she is changed immediately. Then she uses this same tie point to reach others. "Come and meet a man who told me all I ever did!" She proclaims it loudly. Being real with Jesus and with herself has suddenly set her free. *Jesus knows her. Jesus understands her. She wants others to know Jesus, too.*

Carrie also lived in quiet shame. She kept her secret from her mom, her best friend, her youth pastor, and her cheerleading coach. She had even managed to dodge her boyfriend's questions. The only one who knew was the cab driver who had driven her home from the abortion clinic. Carrie had convinced herself that if she could just take care of the "problem" on her own, no one would ever have to know.

Months passed. Though she didn't have to deal with the disappointment and judgment of others, she had never felt so alone and empty. One night, while she was curled up, crying on the bathroom floor, Jesus made Himself known to Carrie. In the midst of her tears and loneliness, Jesus invaded her story by simply whispering to her, "I know." She couldn't keep her secret from God. Unconditional love poured into her empty life. Being known was not nearly as painful as being alone. God's Story connected to her story and it brought freedom instead of shame. Jesus not only forgave her, He also gave her the strength to tell her story to those closest to her. Twenty-five years later, Carrie continues to be free, and she invites girls with a similar story to "come and meet the man who knows all I ever did."

When you receive God's unconditional love, it connects God's Story to your story. When you offer unconditional love, it connects your story to your friend's story. The story of Jesus' encounter with the woman at the well leaves us with great direction for living an authentic Christian life.

>> Know that God's love frees you to be real with others.
>> Model unconditional love.
>> Leave the "well" where Jesus meets you and invite your friends to meet the One who knows all you ever did.

the Samaritans came to him, they asked him to stay with them, and he stayed there two days. **41** And many more believed because of his word. **42** They said to the woman, "It is no longer because of what you said that we believe, for we have heard for ourselves, and we know that this is indeed the Savior of the world."

43 After the two days he departed for Galilee. **44** (For Jesus himself had testified that a prophet has no honor in his own hometown.) **45** So when he came to Galilee, the Galileans welcomed him, having seen all that he had done in Jerusalem at the feast. For they too had gone to the feast.

Jesus Heals an Official's Son

46 So he came again to Cana in Galilee, where he had made the water wine. And at Capernaum there was an official whose son was ill. **47** When this man heard that Jesus had come from Judea to Galilee, he went to him and asked him to come down and heal his son, for he was at the point of death. **48** So Jesus said to him, "Unless you see signs and wonders you will not believe." **49** The official said to him, "Sir, come down before my child dies." **50** Jesus said to him, "Go; your son will live." The man believed the word that Jesus spoke to him and went on his way. **51** As he was going down, his servants[1] met him and told him that his son was recovering. **52** So he asked them the hour when he began to get better, and they said to him, "Yesterday at the seventh hour[2] the fever left him." **53** The father

---

1 Greek *bondservants*   2 That is, at 1 P.M.

knew that was the hour when Jesus had said to him, "Your son will live." And he himself believed, and all his household. [54]This was now the second sign that Jesus did when he had come from Judea to Galilee.

The Healing at the Pool on the Sabbath

5 After this there was a feast of the Jews, and Jesus went up to Jerusalem.

[2]Now there is in Jerusalem by the Sheep Gate a pool, in Aramaic[1] called Bethesda,[2] which has five roofed colonnades. [3]In these lay a multitude of invalids—blind, lame, and paralyzed.[3] [5]One man was there who had been an invalid for thirty-eight years. [6]When Jesus saw him lying there and knew that he had already been there a long time, he said to him, "Do you want to be healed?" [7]The sick man answered him, "Sir, I have no one to put me into the pool when the water is stirred up, and while I am going another steps down before me." [8]Jesus said to him, "Get up, take up your bed, and walk." [9]And at once the man was healed, and he took up his bed and walked.

Now that day was the Sabbath. [10]So the Jews said to the man who had been healed, "It is the Sabbath, and it is not lawful for you to take up your bed." [11]But he answered them, "The man who healed me, that man said to me, 'Take up your bed, and walk.'" [12]They asked him, "Who is the man who said to you, 'Take up your bed and walk'?" [13]Now the man who had been healed did not know who it was, for

---

1 Or *Hebrew* 2 Some manuscripts *Bethsaida* 3 Some manuscripts insert, wholly or in part, *waiting for the moving of the water*; *4 for an angel of the Lord went down at certain seasons into the pool, and stirred the water: whoever stepped in first after the stirring of the water was healed of whatever disease he had*

Jesus had withdrawn, as there was a crowd in the place. [14] Afterward Jesus found him in the temple and said to him, "See, you are well! Sin no more, that nothing worse may happen to you." [15] The man went away and told the Jews that it was Jesus who had healed him. [16] And this was why the Jews were persecuting Jesus, because he was doing these things on the Sabbath. [17] But Jesus answered them, "My Father is working until now, and I am working."

Jesus Is Equal with God

[18] This was why the Jews were seeking all the more to kill him, because not only was he breaking the Sabbath, but he was even calling God his own Father, making himself equal with God.

The Authority of the Son

[19] So Jesus said to them, "Truly, truly, I say to you, the Son can do nothing of his own accord, but only what he sees the Father doing. For whatever the Father[1] does, that the Son does likewise. [20] For the Father loves the Son and shows him all that he himself is doing. And greater works than these will he show him, so that you may marvel. [21] For as the Father raises the dead and gives them life, so also the Son gives life to whom he will. [22] The Father judges no one, but has given all judgment to the Son, [23] that all may honor the Son, just as they honor the Father. Whoever does not honor the Son does not honor the Father who sent him. [24] Truly, truly, I say to you, whoever

[1] Greek *he*

hears my word and believes him who sent me has eternal life. He does not come into judgment, but has passed from death to life.

²⁵ "Truly, truly, I say to you, an hour is coming, and is now here, when the dead will hear the voice of the Son of God, and those who hear will live. ²⁶ For as the Father has life in himself, so he has granted the Son also to have life in himself. ²⁷ And he has given him authority to execute judgment, because he is the Son of Man. ²⁸ Do not marvel at this, for an hour is coming when all who are in the tombs will hear his voice ²⁹ and come out, those who have done good to the resurrection of life, and those who have done evil to the resurrection of judgment.

Witnesses to Jesus

³⁰ "I can do nothing on my own. As I hear, I judge, and my judgment is just, because I seek not my own will but the will of him who sent me. ³¹ If I alone bear witness about myself, my testimony is not deemed true. ³² There is another who bears witness about me, and I know that the testimony that he bears about me is true. ³³ You sent to John, and he has borne witness to the truth. ³⁴ Not that the testimony that I receive is from man, but I say these things so that you may be saved. ³⁵ He was a burning and shining lamp, and you were willing to rejoice for a while in his light. ³⁶ But the testimony that I have is greater than that of John. For the works that the Father has given me to accomplish, the very works that I am doing, bear witness about me that the Father has sent me. ³⁷ And the Father who sent me has

The Lame Man

>>TIRED OF WAITING

I watched her stooped over, leaning on her walker. Her slow steps and the look on her face told me each movement was painful. She was my neighbor, and I had seen her pass in front of my house more times than I could count. Some days I found it difficult to watch her, and other days I couldn't help but stare out the window and wonder how she kept going. My neighbor's goal was the corner store to make her daily purchases. More than once I had stopped her and asked if I could give her a ride or go to the store for her or carry her packages. Each time she would reply, "If I let you help me now, who will help me tomorrow? I am better off doing it on my own."

The lame man Jesus met at the pool must have felt something like my neighbor lady. *I don't have anyone to help me. It is up to me to get what I need.* His goal was being healed. The pool of Bethesda was his only hope.

This man was one of many in the crowd, and Jesus chose this moment to meet him where he was. Knowing he had been waiting a long time, Jesus used a gentle tug: "Do you want to be healed?" The man responded to Jesus with excuses: "I don't have anyone to help me. Every time I try, someone else gets there first." Jesus ignored the excuses and challenged the man, "Get up, take up your bed, and walk."

It was a life-changing decision.

Would he refuse the help (much like my neighbor lady did) and continue to live with his excuses and pain? Desperate to be healed, he did what he had not been able to do for thirty-eight years. That is, he got up and walked. He was healed, but he was not yet saying yes to Jesus. This was his first encounter with the Messiah. The need for healing was the man's doorway, and he was just beginning the journey to understand how much more Jesus was offering him.

Both my neighbor and the lame man provide excellent examples of how your friends may respond to Jesus. Some will absolutely refuse the help you and Jesus offer, choosing to stay in their pain. You may have to watch them struggle every day and keep offering help.

Your friends may respond as the lame man did, making excuses like these for why they cannot trust Jesus:

>> I do not want to give up partying on Friday nights.

>> I need to get my life straightened out first.

>> I am not that bad of a person.

>> Jesus is for weak people who cannot stand on their own. I don't need Him.

Still other friends may say yes to help, even before they put their trust in God.

The amazing part of Jesus' encounters is that He meets people where they are and He is never offended by their responses or slowed down by their excuses. Often we grow frustrated when our friends are unresponsive or when our gentle tugs do not seem to work. God's Story can bring healing and new life to your friend, yet it is always in His own time. Your role is to keep meeting your friends where they are and keep disclosing your story and discovering Their Story.

Consider one friend who is on your Wish List. (See p. xviii for the explanation of the Wish List.)

>> Are you meeting this person where he or she is?

>> Are you being real with him or her?

>> Are you listening well?

>> Does this person feel loved by you?

>> What gentle tug could you try?

Take a moment right now and pray for your friend.

himself borne witness about me. His voice you have never heard, his form you have never seen, [38] and you do not have his word abiding in you, for you do not believe the one whom he has sent. [39] You search the Scriptures because you think that in them you have eternal life; and it is they that bear witness about me, [40] yet you refuse to come to me that you may have life. [41] I do not receive glory from people. [42] But I know that you do not have the love of God within you. [43] I have come in my Father's name, and you do not receive me. If another comes in his own name, you will receive him. [44] How can you believe, when you receive glory from one another and do not seek the glory that comes from the only God? [45] Do not think that I will accuse you to the Father. There is one who accuses you: Moses, on whom you have set your hope. [46] If you believed Moses, you would believe me; for he wrote of me. [47] But if you do not believe his writings, how will you believe my words?"

Jesus Feeds the Five Thousand

After this [a] Jesus went away to the other side of the Sea of Galilee, which is the Sea of Tiberias. [2] And a large crowd was following him, because they saw the signs that he was doing on the sick. [3] Jesus went up on the mountain, and there he sat down with his disciples. [4] Now the Passover, the feast of the Jews, was at hand. [5] Lifting up his eyes, then, and seeing that a large crowd was coming toward him, Jesus said to Philip, "Where are we to buy bread, so that these people may eat?" [6] He said this to test him, for

a For 6:1-13 see parallels Matt. 14:13-21; Mark 6:32-44; Luke 9:10-17 he himself knew what he would do. [7] Philip answered him, "Two hundred denarii[1] would not buy enough bread for each of them to get a little." [8] One of his disciples, Andrew, Simon Peter's brother, said to him, [9] "There is a boy here who has five barley loaves and two fish, but what are they for so many?" [10] Jesus said, "Have the people sit down." Now there was much grass in the place. So the men sat down, about five thousand in number. [11] Jesus then took the loaves, and when he had given thanks, he distributed them to those who were seated. So also the fish, as much as they wanted. [12] And when they had eaten their fill, he told his disciples, "Gather up the leftover fragments, that nothing may be lost." [13] So they gathered them up and filled twelve baskets with fragments from the five barley loaves, left by those who had eaten. [14] When the people saw the sign that he had done, they said, "This is indeed the Prophet who is to come into the world!"

[15] Perceiving then that they were about to come and take him by force to make him king, Jesus *a* withdrew again to the mountain by himself.

Jesus Walks on Water

[16] When evening came, his disciples went down to the sea, [17] got into a boat, and started across the sea to Capernaum. It was now dark, and Jesus had not yet come to them. [18] The sea became rough because a strong wind was blowing. [19] When they had rowed about three or four miles,[2] they saw Jesus walking on the sea and coming

---

[1] A *denarius* was a day's wage for a laborer [2] Greek *twenty-five or thirty stadia*; a *stadion* was about 607 feet or 185 meters [a] For 6:15-21 see parallels Matt. 14:22-33; Mark 6:45-52

near the boat, and they were frightened. ²⁰ But he said to them, "It is I; do not be afraid." ²¹ Then they were glad to take him into the boat, and immediately the boat was at the land to which they were going.

I Am the Bread of Life

²² On the next day the crowd that remained on the other side of the sea saw that there had been only one boat there, and that Jesus had not entered the boat with his disciples, but that his disciples had gone away alone. ²³ Other boats from Tiberias came near the place where they had eaten the bread after the Lord had given thanks. ²⁴ So when the crowd saw that Jesus was not there, nor his disciples, they themselves got into the boats and went to Capernaum, seeking Jesus.

²⁵ When they found him on the other side of the sea, they said to him, "Rabbi, when did you come here?" ²⁶ Jesus answered them, "Truly, truly, I say to you, you are seeking me, not because you saw signs, but because you ate your fill of the loaves. ²⁷ Do not labor for the food that perishes, but for the food that endures to eternal life, which the Son of Man will give to you. For on him God the Father has set his seal." ²⁸ Then they said to him, "What must we do, to be doing the works of God?" ²⁹ Jesus answered them, "This is the work of God, that you believe in him whom he has sent." ³⁰ So they said to him, "Then what sign do you do, that we may see and believe you? What work do you perform? ³¹ Our fathers ate the manna in the wilderness; as it is written, *a*'He gave them bread from heaven to

a Neh. 9:15

eat.'" ³² Jesus then said to them, "Truly, truly, I say to you, it was not Moses who gave you the bread from heaven, but my Father gives you the true bread from heaven. ³³ For the bread of God is he who comes down from heaven and gives life to the world." ³⁴ They said to him, "Sir, give us this bread always."

³⁵ Jesus said to them, "I am the bread of life; whoever comes to me shall not hunger, and whoever believes in me shall never thirst. ³⁶ But I said to you that you have seen me and yet do not believe. ³⁷ All that the Father gives me will come to me, and whoever comes to me I will never cast out. ³⁸ For I have come down from heaven, not to do my own will but the will of him who sent me. ³⁹ And this is the will of him who sent me, that I should lose nothing of all that he has given me, but raise it up on the last day. ⁴⁰ For this is the will of my Father, that everyone who looks on the Son and believes in him should have eternal life, and I will raise him up on the last day."

⁴¹ So the Jews grumbled about him, because he said, "I am the bread that came down from heaven." ⁴² They said, "Is not this Jesus, the son of Joseph, whose father and mother we know? How does he now say, 'I have come down from heaven'?" ⁴³ Jesus answered them, "Do not grumble among yourselves. ⁴⁴ No one can come to me unless the Father who sent me draws him. And I will raise him up on the last day. ⁴⁵ It is written in the Prophets, ᵃ 'And they will all be taught by God.' Everyone who has heard and learned from the Father comes to me— ⁴⁶ not that anyone has seen the Father except he who is from God; he has seen the Father. ⁴⁷ Truly, truly, I say to you, whoever believes has eternal life. ⁴⁸ I am the bread of

life. 49 Your fathers ate the manna in the wilderness, and they died. 50 This is the bread that comes down from heaven, so that one may eat of it and not die. 51 I am the living bread that came down from heaven. If anyone eats of this bread, he will live forever. And the bread that I will give for the life of the world is my flesh."

52 The Jews then disputed among themselves, saying, "How can this man give us his flesh to eat?" 53 So Jesus said to them, "Truly, truly, I say to you, unless you eat the flesh of the Son of Man and drink his blood, you have no life in you. 54 Whoever feeds on my flesh and drinks my blood has eternal life, and I will raise him up on the last day. 55 For my flesh is true food, and my blood is true drink. 56 Whoever feeds on my flesh and drinks my blood abides in me, and I in him. 57 As the living Father sent me, and I live because of the Father, so whoever feeds on me, he also will live because of me. 58 This is the bread that came down from heaven, not as the fathers ate and died. Whoever feeds on this bread will live forever." 59 Jesus[1] said these things in the synagogue, as he taught at Capernaum.

The Words of Eternal Life

60 When many of his disciples heard it, they said, "This is a hard saying; who can listen to it?" 61 But Jesus, knowing in himself that his disciples were grumbling about this, said to them, "Do you take offense at this? 62 Then what if you were to see the Son of Man ascending to where he was before? 63 It is the Spirit who gives life; the flesh is of no avail. The words that I have spoken to you are spirit

1 Greek *He*

and life. ⁶⁴But there are some of you who do not believe." (For Jesus knew from the beginning who those were who did not believe, and who it was who would betray him.) ⁶⁵ And he said, "This is why I told you that no one can come to me unless it is granted him by the Father."

⁶⁶ After this many of his disciples turned back and no longer walked with him. ⁶⁷ So Jesus said to the Twelve, "Do you want to go away as well?" ⁶⁸ Simon Peter answered him, "Lord, to whom shall we go? You have the words of eternal life, ⁶⁹ and we have believed, and have come to know, that you are the Holy One of God." ⁷⁰ Jesus answered them, "Did I not choose you, the Twelve? And yet one of you is a devil." ⁷¹ He spoke of Judas the son of Simon Iscariot, for he, one of the Twelve, was going to betray him.

Jesus at the Feast of Booths

After this Jesus went about in Galilee. He would not go about in Judea, because the Jews[1] were seeking to kill him. ² Now the Jews' Feast of Booths was at hand. ³ So his brothers[2] said to him, "Leave here and go to Judea, that your disciples also may see the works you are doing. ⁴ For no one works in secret if he seeks to be known openly. If you do these things, show yourself to the world." ⁵ For not even his brothers believed in him. ⁶ Jesus said to them, "My time has not yet come, but your time is always here. ⁷ The world cannot hate you, but it hates me because I testify about it that its works are evil. ⁸ You go up to the feast. I am not[3] going up

1 Or *Judeans* 2 Or *brothers and sisters*; also verses 5, 10 3 Some manuscripts add *yet*

to this feast, for my time has not yet fully come." ⁹ After saying this, he remained in Galilee.

¹⁰ But after his brothers had gone up to the feast, then he also went up, not publicly but in private. ¹¹ The Jews were looking for him at the feast, and saying, "Where is he?" ¹² And there was much muttering about him among the people. While some said, "He is a good man," others said, "No, he is leading the people astray." ¹³ Yet for fear of the Jews no one spoke openly of him.

¹⁴ About the middle of the feast Jesus went up into the temple and began teaching. ¹⁵ The Jews therefore marveled, saying, "How is it that this man has learning,[1] when he has never studied?" ¹⁶ So Jesus answered them, "My teaching is not mine, but his who sent me. ¹⁷ If anyone's will is to do God's[2] will, he will know whether the teaching is from God or whether I am speaking on my own authority. ¹⁸ The one who speaks on his own authority seeks his own glory, but the one who seeks the glory of him who sent him is true, and in him there is no falsehood. ¹⁹ Has not Moses given you the law? Yet none of you keeps the law. Why do you seek to kill me?" ²⁰ The crowd answered, "You have a demon! Who is seeking to kill you?" ²¹ Jesus answered them, "I did one deed, and you all marvel at it. ²² Moses gave you circumcision (not that it is from Moses, but from the fathers), and you circumcise a man on the Sabbath. ²³ If on the Sabbath a man receives circumcision, so that the law of Moses may not be broken, are you angry with me because on the Sabbath I made a man's whole body well? ²⁴ Do not judge by appearances, but judge with right judgment."

1 Or *this man knows his letters*   2 Greek *his*

Can This Be the Christ?

²⁵ Some of the people of Jerusalem therefore said, "Is not this the man whom they seek to kill? ²⁶ And here he is, speaking openly, and they say nothing to him! Can it be that the authorities really know that this is the Christ? ²⁷ But we know where this man comes from, and when the Christ appears, no one will know where he comes from." ²⁸ So Jesus proclaimed, as he taught in the temple, "You know me, and you know where I come from? But I have not come of my own accord. He who sent me is true, and him you do not know. ²⁹ I know him, for I come from him, and he sent me." ³⁰ So they were seeking to arrest him, but no one laid a hand on him, because his hour had not yet come. ³¹ Yet many of the people believed in him. They said, "When the Christ appears, will he do more signs than this man has done?"

Officers Sent to Arrest Jesus

³² The Pharisees heard the crowd muttering these things about him, and the chief priests and Pharisees sent officers to arrest him. ³³ Jesus then said, "I will be with you a little longer, and then I am going to him who sent me. ³⁴ You will seek me and you will not find me. Where I am you cannot come." ³⁵ The Jews said to one another, "Where does this man intend to go that we will not find him? Does he intend to go to the Dispersion among the Greeks and teach the

Greeks? ³⁶ What does he mean by saying, 'You will seek me and you will not find me,' and, 'Where I am you cannot come'?"

Rivers of Living Water

³⁷ On the last day of the feast, the great day, Jesus stood up and cried out, "If anyone thirsts, let him come to me and drink. ³⁸ Whoever believes in me, as[1] the Scripture has said, 'Out of his heart will flow rivers of living water.'" ³⁹ Now this he said about the Spirit, whom those who believed in him were to receive, for as yet the Spirit had not been given, because Jesus was not yet glorified.

Division Among the People

⁴⁰ When they heard these words, some of the people said, "This really is the Prophet." ⁴¹ Others said, "This is the Christ." But some said, "Is the Christ to come from Galilee? ⁴² Has not the Scripture said that the Christ comes from the offspring of David, and comes from Bethlehem, the village where David was?" ⁴³ So there was a division among the people over him. ⁴⁴ Some of them wanted to arrest him, but no one laid hands on him.

⁴⁵ The officers then came to the chief priests and Pharisees, who said to them, "Why did you not bring him?" ⁴⁶ The officers answered, "No one ever spoke like this man!" ⁴⁷ The Pharisees answered them, "Have you also been deceived? ⁴⁸ Have any of the authorities or the Pharisees believed in him? ⁴⁹ But this crowd that does not know

1 Or *let him come to me, and let him who believes in me drink. As*

the law is accursed." 50 Nicodemus, who had gone to him before, and who was one of them, said to them, 51 "Does our law judge a man without first giving him a hearing and learning what he does?" 52 They replied, "Are you from Galilee too? Search and see that no prophet arises from Galilee."

[THE EARLIEST MANUSCRIPTS DO NOT
INCLUDE JOHN 7:53–8:11][1]

The Woman Caught in Adultery

53 [[They went each to his own house,1 but Jesus went to the Mount of Olives. 2 Early in the morning he came again to the temple. All the people came to him, and he sat down and taught them. 3 The scribes and the Pharisees brought a woman who had been caught in adultery, and placing her in the midst 4 they said to him, "Teacher, this woman has been caught in the act of adultery. 5 Now in the Law Moses commanded us to stone such women. So what do you say?" 6 This they said to test him, that they might have some charge to bring against him. Jesus bent down and wrote with his finger on the ground. 7 And as they continued to ask him, he stood up and said to them, "Let him who is without sin among you be the first to throw a stone at her." 8 And once more he bent down and wrote on the ground. 9 But when they heard it, they went away one by one, beginning with the older ones, and Jesus was left alone with the woman standing before him.

1 Some manuscripts do not include 7:53–8:11; others add the passage here or after 7:36 or after 21:25 or after Luke 21:38, with variations in the text

The Woman Caught in Adultery

>>CAUGHT IN THE ACT!

Did you ever get caught in an embarrassing situation? The woman in this story sure did. But without many of the specifics, we are left with lots of unanswered questions.

>> What was this woman's story?

>> How did she end up in bed with a man to whom she wasn't married?

>> How was she discovered?

>> What happened to the guy?

>> Did the woman think she was about to die?

What we do know is that she was caught in the act of adultery, and the religious leaders were ready and willing to kill her without even hearing her story.

People enjoy pointing out the wrong in others! Even Christians sometimes show too much judgment and too little grace to a person struggling with sin. Does that sound a lot like what happens at your school? Like when:

>> You talk about the football pass the tight end dropped more than the five he caught.

>> By Monday everyone knows every detail of every weekend party.

>> Your nickname highlights a physical trait you can't change.

>> Racial or social stereotypes leave you out of the "in" crowd.

>> Friends are more concerned about spreading gossip than helping the person about whom they are gossiping.

As a 3Story student, you can go against the crowd and stick up for students who are unfairly rejected. You can be the one who doesn't judge students who are caught in the act and even arrested, suspended from school, or kicked out of the house. When you make a mistake (and everyone does), wouldn't it be nice if someone just loved you anyway? That is what Jesus did for this woman, and that is what you can do, too.

One of the high points of God's Story is that He loves us even when we all resist Him. We tend to run off and do what we know is wrong. The Bible calls that sin and says, "All have sinned and fall short of the glory of God" (Romans 3:23). Although we don't know what Jesus wrote in the sand in front of the crowd, his pointed statement showed the religious leaders that they were sinners. And Jesus did not want the woman to continue sinning either.

When you become aware of sin in your life, Jesus expects you to change! Stop trying to hide your sin. Stop living in fear of getting "caught in the act." Think of the sin that keeps tripping you up. Jesus says you can make the choice to "sin no more."

Thank God for the tremendous truth that we learn from this brief encounter between Jesus and a very scared woman. That truth is: *Jesus knows My Story and loves me anyway. He doesn't see me for what I have done in the past. He sees me for who I can be and what I can do in the future.*

¹⁰ Jesus stood up and said to her, "Woman, where are they? Has no one condemned you?" ¹¹ She said, "No one, Lord." And Jesus said, "Neither do I condemn you; go, and from now on sin no more."]]

I Am the Light of the World

¹² Again Jesus spoke to them, saying, "I am the light of the world. Whoever follows me will not walk in darkness, but will have the light of life." ¹³ So the Pharisees said to him, "You are bearing witness about yourself; your testimony is not true." ¹⁴ Jesus answered, "Even if I do bear witness about myself, my testimony is true, for I know where I came from and where I am going, but you do not know where I come from or where I am going. ¹⁵ You judge according to the flesh; I judge no one. ¹⁶ Yet even if I do judge, my judgment is true, for it is not I alone who judge, but I and the Father[1] who sent me. ¹⁷ In your Law it is written that the testimony of two men is true. ¹⁸ I am the one who bears witness about myself, and the Father who sent me bears witness about me." ¹⁹ They said to him therefore, "Where is your Father?" Jesus answered, "You know neither me nor my Father. If you knew me, you would know my Father also." ²⁰ These words he spoke in the treasury, as he taught in the temple; but no one arrested him, because his hour had not yet come.

²¹ So he said to them again, "I am going away, and you will seek me, and you will die in your sin. Where I am going, you cannot come." ²² So the Jews said, "Will he kill himself, since he says, 'Where I am going, you cannot come'?" ²³ He said to them, "You are

---

1 Some manuscripts *he*

from below; I am from above. You are of this world; I am not of this world. 24 I told you that you would die in your sins, for unless you believe that I am he you will die in your sins." 25 So they said to him, "Who are you?" Jesus said to them, "Just what I have been telling you from the beginning. 26 I have much to say about you and much to judge, but he who sent me is true, and I declare to the world what I have heard from him." 27 They did not understand that he had been speaking to them about the Father. 28 So Jesus said to them, "When you have lifted up the Son of Man, then you will know that I am he, and that I do nothing on my own authority, but speak just as the Father taught me. 29 And he who sent me is with me. He has not left me alone, for I always do the things that are pleasing to him." 30 As he was saying these things, many believed in him.

The Truth Will Set You Free

31 So Jesus said to the Jews who had believed in him, "If you abide in my word, you are truly my disciples, 32 and you will know the truth, and the truth will set you free." 33 They answered him, "We are offspring of Abraham and have never been enslaved to anyone. How is it that you say, 'You will become free'?"

34 Jesus answered them, "Truly, truly, I say to you, everyone who commits sin is a slave [1] to sin. 35 The slave does not remain in the house forever; the son remains forever. 36 So if the Son sets you free, you will be free indeed. 37 I know that you are offspring of Abraham; yet you seek to kill me because my word finds no place in you.

1 Greek bondservant; also verse 35

³⁸ I speak of what I have seen with my Father, and you do what you have heard from your father."

You Are of Your Father the Devil

³⁹ They answered him, "Abraham is our father." Jesus said to them, "If you were Abraham's children, you would be doing what Abraham did, ⁴⁰ but now you seek to kill me, a man who has told you the truth that I heard from God. This is not what Abraham did. ⁴¹ You are doing what your father did." They said to him, "We were not born of sexual immorality. We have one Father—even God." ⁴² Jesus said to them, "If God were your Father, you would love me, for I came from God and I am here. I came not of my own accord, but he sent me. ⁴³ Why do you not understand what I say? It is because you cannot bear to hear my word. ⁴⁴ You are of your father the devil, and your will is to do your father's desires. He was a murderer from the beginning, and has nothing to do with the truth, because there is no truth in him. When he lies, he speaks out of his own character, for he is a liar and the father of lies. ⁴⁵ But because I tell the truth, you do not believe me. ⁴⁶ Which one of you convicts me of sin? If I tell the truth, why do you not believe me? ⁴⁷ Whoever is of God hears the words of God. The reason why you do not hear them is that you are not of God."

Before Abraham Was, I Am

⁴⁸ The Jews answered him, "Are we not right in saying that you are a Samaritan and have a demon?" ⁴⁹ Jesus answered, "I do not have a

demon, but I honor my Father, and you dishonor me. ⁵⁰ Yet I do not seek my own glory; there is One who seeks it, and he is the judge. ⁵¹ Truly, truly, I say to you, if anyone keeps my word, he will never see death." ⁵² The Jews said to him, "Now we know that you have a demon! Abraham died, as did the prophets, yet you say, 'If anyone keeps my word, he will never taste death.' ⁵³ Are you greater than our father Abraham, who died? And the prophets died! Who do you make yourself out to be?" ⁵⁴ Jesus answered, "If I glorify myself, my glory is nothing. It is my Father who glorifies me, of whom you say, 'He is our God.'[1] ⁵⁵ But you have not known him. I know him. If I were to say that I do not know him, I would be a liar like you, but I do know him and I keep his word. ⁵⁶ Your father Abraham rejoiced that he would see my day. He saw it and was glad." ⁵⁷ So the Jews said to him, "You are not yet fifty years old, and have you seen Abraham?"[2] ⁵⁸ Jesus said to them, "Truly, truly, I say to you, before Abraham was, I am." ⁵⁹ So they picked up stones to throw at him, but Jesus hid himself and went out of the temple.

Jesus Heals a Man Born Blind

As he passed by, he saw a man blind from birth. ² And his disciples asked him, "Rabbi, who sinned, this man or his parents, that he was born blind?" ³ Jesus answered, "It was not that this man sinned, or his parents, but that the works of God might be displayed in him. ⁴ We must work the works of him who sent me while it is day; night is coming, when no one can work. ⁵ As long as I am in the world, I am the light of the world." ⁶ Having said

1 Some manuscripts *your God*   2 Some manuscripts *has Abraham seen you?*

these things, he spat on the ground and made mud with the saliva. Then he anointed the man's eyes with the mud ⁷ and said to him, "Go, wash in the pool of Siloam" (which means Sent). So he went and washed and came back seeing.

⁸ The neighbors and those who had seen him before as a beggar were saying, "Is this not the man who used to sit and beg?" ⁹ Some said, "It is he." Others said, "No, but he is like him." He kept saying, "I am the man." ¹⁰ So they said to him, "Then how were your eyes opened?" ¹¹ He answered, "The man called Jesus made mud and anointed my eyes and said to me, 'Go to Siloam and wash.' So I went and washed and received my sight." ¹² They said to him, "Where is he?" He said, "I do not know."

¹³ They brought to the Pharisees the man who had formerly been blind. ¹⁴ Now it was a Sabbath day when Jesus made the mud and opened his eyes. ¹⁵ So the Pharisees again asked him how he had received his sight. And he said to them, "He put mud on my eyes, and I washed, and I see." ¹⁶ Some of the Pharisees said, "This man is not from God, for he does not keep the Sabbath." But others said, "How can a man who is a sinner do such signs?" And there was a division among them. ¹⁷ So they said again to the blind man, "What do you say about him, since he has opened your eyes?" He said, "He is a prophet."

¹⁸ The Jews did not believe that he had been blind and had received his sight, until they called the parents of the man who had received his sight ¹⁹ and asked them, "Is this your son, who you say was born blind? How then does he now see?" ²⁰ His parents answered, "We

know that this is our son and that he was born blind. [21]But how he now sees we do not know, nor do we know who opened his eyes. Ask him; he is of age. He will speak for himself." [22](His parents said these things because they feared the Jews, for the Jews had already agreed that if anyone should confess Jesus[1] to be Christ, he was to be put out of the synagogue.) [23]Therefore his parents said, "He is of age; ask him."

[24]So for the second time they called the man who had been blind and said to him, "Give glory to God. We know that this man is a sinner." [25]He answered, "Whether he is a sinner I do not know. One thing I do know, that though I was blind, now I see." [26]They said to him, "What did he do to you? How did he open your eyes?" [27]He answered them, "I have told you already, and you would not listen. Why do you want to hear it again? Do you also want to become his disciples?" [28]And they reviled him, saying, "You are his disciple, but we are disciples of Moses. [29]We know that God has spoken to Moses, but as for this man, we do not know where he comes from." [30]The man answered, "Why, this is an amazing thing! You do not know where he comes from, and yet he opened my eyes. [31]We know that God does not listen to sinners, but if anyone is a worshiper of God and does his will, God listens to him. [32]Never since the world began has it been heard that anyone opened the eyes of a man born blind. [33]If this man were not from God, he could do nothing." [34]They answered him, "You were born in utter sin, and would you teach us?" And they cast him out.

[35]Jesus heard that they had cast him out, and having found him

1 Greek him

JOHN 9:1-41

>>JUST PASSING BY

Everywhere Jesus went, people's lives were changed—even when He was just "passing by." It seems as if Jesus always had time to stop and meet someone's need—this time, it was a man blind from birth. We can only imagine the home remedies and diet supplements this man had tried without success. We don't know if he had heard about Jesus before. He simply knew he suddenly had mud on his eyes, and he might as well play along and go wash it off. He came back seeing and with a new story to tell.

Many of our opportunities to connect My Story to our friends' stories happen as we "pass by" in the school halls or when we're hanging out with them. The change we see in our friends will not often be as dramatic as giving sight to a blind man. The gifts of loving them as they are and listening to their stories, however, open the door for them to "see" Jesus differently.

Like the disciples, most of us wonder why bad things happen to good people in the first place. Notice that Jesus didn't offer a deep, medical explanation, nor did He teach that God punishes us by sending us some random health problem. Jesus taught that even in the midst of the tough situations we face in life, the "works of God might be displayed." God will help us deal with any issue we must face when we connect to His story.

You will be excited to see changes in your friends' lives, but don't be surprised when some people aren't sure what to think. The spiritual blindness shown by the religious leaders is still common in our world. Instead of trying to understand God's Story, some people avoid Jesus by making statements like these:

>> All religions worship the same God.

>> A loving God wouldn't send anyone to hell.

>> I can't believe in God and science at the same time.

>> Christians are judgmental and intolerant.

>> People just use religion as a crutch.

The man born blind simply knew the difference that Jesus had made in his life. He stated, "One thing I do know, that though I was blind, now I see." Sometimes we can't explain everything that has happened in us, but we know our relationship with Jesus has made it possible. When it comes to disclosing My Story, simply share how your life is different since you decided to follow Jesus.

What are three changes God has made in your life? List them here and thank Him for "passing by" your life. Remember to include these when you share your story.

1. _____

_____

2. _____

_____

3. _____

_____

You may not have all the answers to your friends' questions, but you are a great example of what can happen when Jesus passes by! Don't be afraid to share the "one thing" that you know!

he said, "Do you believe in the Son of Man?" [1] ³⁶He answered, "And who is he, sir, that I may believe in him?" ³⁷Jesus said to him, "You have seen him, and it is he who is speaking to you." ³⁸He said, "Lord, I believe," and he worshiped him. ³⁹Jesus said, "For judgment I came into this world, that those who do not see may see, and those who see may become blind." ⁴⁰Some of the Pharisees near him heard these things, and said to him, "Are we also blind?" ⁴¹Jesus said to them, "If you were blind, you would have no guilt; [2] but now that you say, 'We see,' your guilt remains.

I Am the Good Shepherd

10 "Truly, truly, I say to you, he who does not enter the sheepfold by the door but climbs in by another way, that man is a thief and a robber. ²But he who enters by the door is the shepherd of the sheep. ³To him the gatekeeper opens. The sheep hear his voice, and he calls his own sheep by name and leads them out. ⁴When he has brought out all his own, he goes before them, and the sheep follow him, for they know his voice. ⁵A stranger they will not follow, but they will flee from him, for they do not know the voice of strangers." ⁶This figure of speech Jesus used with them, but they did not understand what he was saying to them.

⁷So Jesus again said to them, "Truly, truly, I say to you, I am the door of the sheep. ⁸All who came before me are thieves and robbers, but the sheep did not listen to them. ⁹I am the door. If anyone enters

1 Some manuscripts *the Son of God* 2 Greek *you would not have sin*

by me, he will be saved and will go in and out and find pasture. [10]The thief comes only to steal and kill and destroy. I came that they may have life and have it abundantly. [11]I am the good shepherd. The good shepherd lays down his life for the sheep. [12]He who is a hired hand and not a shepherd, who does not own the sheep, sees the wolf coming and leaves the sheep and flees, and the wolf snatches them and scatters them. [13]He flees because he is a hired hand and cares nothing for the sheep. [14]I am the good shepherd. I know my own and my own know me, [15]just as the Father knows me and I know the Father; and I lay down my life for the sheep. [16]And I have other sheep that are not of this fold. I must bring them also, and they will listen to my voice. So there will be one flock, one shepherd. [17]For this reason the Father loves me, because I lay down my life that I may take it up again. [18]No one takes it from me, but I lay it down of my own accord. I have authority to lay it down, and I have authority to take it up again. This charge I have received from my Father."

[19]There was again a division among the Jews because of these words. [20]Many of them said, "He has a demon, and is insane; why listen to him?" [21]Others said, "These are not the words of one who is oppressed by a demon. Can a demon open the eyes of the blind?"

I and the Father Are One

[22]At that time the Feast of Dedication took place at Jerusalem. It was winter, [23]and Jesus was walking in the temple, in the colonnade of Solomon. [24]So the Jews gathered around him and said to him,

"How long will you keep us in suspense? If you are the Christ, tell us plainly." 25Jesus answered them, "I told you, and you do not believe. The works that I do in my Father's name bear witness about me, 26but you do not believe because you are not part of my flock. 27My sheep hear my voice, and I know them, and they follow me. 28I give them eternal life, and they will never perish, and no one will snatch them out of my hand. 29My Father, who has given them to me,[1] is greater than all, and no one is able to snatch them out of the Father's hand. 30I and the Father are one."

31The Jews picked up stones again to stone him. 32Jesus answered them, "I have shown you many good works from the Father; for which of them are you going to stone me?" 33The Jews answered him, "It is not for a good work that we are going to stone you but for blasphemy, because you, being a man, make yourself God." 34Jesus answered them, "Is it not written in your Law, a'I said, you are gods'? 35If he called them gods to whom the word of God came—and Scripture cannot be broken— 36do you say of him whom the Father consecrated and sent into the world, 'You are blaspheming,' because I said, 'I am the Son of God'? 37If I am not doing the works of my Father, then do not believe me; 38but if I do them, even though you do not believe me, believe the works, that you may know and understand that the Father is in me and I am in the Father." 39Again they sought to arrest him, but he escaped from their hands.

40He went away again across the Jordan to the place where John had been baptizing at first, and there he remained. 41And many came to him. And they said, "John did no sign, but everything that

---

1 Some manuscripts *What my Father has given to me*   a Ps. 82:6

John said about this man was true." **42**And many believed in him there.

The Death of Lazarus

11 Now a certain man was ill, Lazarus of Bethany, the village of Mary and her sister Martha. **2**It was Mary who anointed the Lord with ointment and wiped his feet with her hair, whose brother Lazarus was ill. **3**So the sisters sent to him, saying, "Lord, he whom you love is ill." **4**But when Jesus heard it he said, "This illness does not lead to death. It is for the glory of God, so that the Son of God may be glorified through it."

5Now Jesus loved Martha and her sister and Lazarus. **6**So, when he heard that Lazarus[1] was ill, he stayed two days longer in the place where he was. **7**Then after this he said to the disciples, "Let us go to Judea again." **8**The disciples said to him, "Rabbi, the Jews were just now seeking to stone you, and are you going there again?" **9**Jesus answered, "Are there not twelve hours in the day? If anyone walks in the day, he does not stumble, because he sees the light of this world. **10**But if anyone walks in the night, he stumbles, because the light is not in him." **11**After saying these things, he said to them, "Our friend Lazarus has fallen asleep, but I go to awaken him." **12**The disciples said to him, "Lord, if he has fallen asleep, he will recover." **13**Now Jesus had spoken of his death, but they thought that he meant taking rest in sleep. **14**Then Jesus told them plainly, "Lazarus has died, **15**and for your sake I am glad that I was not there, so that you may

1 Greek *he*; also verse 17

believe. But let us go to him." [16]So Thomas, called the Twin,[1] said to his fellow disciples, "Let us also go, that we may die with him."

I Am the Resurrection and the Life

[17]Now when Jesus came, he found that Lazarus had already been in the tomb four days. [18]Bethany was near Jerusalem, about two miles[2] off, [19]and many of the Jews had come to Martha and Mary to console them concerning their brother. [20]So when Martha heard that Jesus was coming, she went and met him, but Mary remained seated in the house. [21]Martha said to Jesus, "Lord, if you had been here, my brother would not have died. [22]But even now I know that whatever you ask from God, God will give you." [23]Jesus said to her, "Your brother will rise again." [24]Martha said to him, "I know that he will rise again in the resurrection on the last day." [25]Jesus said to her, "I am the resurrection and the life.[3] Whoever believes in me, though he die, yet shall he live, [26]and everyone who lives and believes in me shall never die. Do you believe this?" [27]She said to him, "Yes, Lord; I believe that you are the Christ, the Son of God, who is coming into the world."

Jesus Wept

[28]When she had said this, she went and called her sister Mary, saying in private, "The Teacher is here and is calling for you." [29]And when she heard it, she rose quickly and went to him. [30]Now Jesus had

---

1 Greek *Didymus* 2 Greek *fifteen stadia; a stadion* was about 607 feet or 185 meters 3 Some manuscripts omit *and the life*

not yet come into the village, but was still in the place where Martha had met him. ³¹When the Jews who were with her in the house, consoling her, saw Mary rise quickly and go out, they followed her, supposing that she was going to the tomb to weep there. ³²Now when Mary came to where Jesus was and saw him, she fell at his feet, saying to him, "Lord, if you had been here, my brother would not have died." ³³When Jesus saw her weeping, and the Jews who had come with her also weeping, he was deeply moved in his spirit and greatly troubled. ³⁴And he said, "Where have you laid him?" They said to him, "Lord, come and see." ³⁵Jesus wept. ³⁶So the Jews said, "See how he loved him!" ³⁷But some of them said, "Could not he who opened the eyes of the blind man also have kept this man from dying?"

Jesus Raises Lazarus

³⁸Then Jesus, deeply moved again, came to the tomb. It was a cave, and a stone lay against it. ³⁹Jesus said, "Take away the stone." Martha, the sister of the dead man, said to him, "Lord, by this time there will be an odor, for he has been dead four days." ⁴⁰Jesus said to her, "Did I not tell you that if you believed you would see the glory of God?" ⁴¹So they took away the stone. And Jesus lifted up his eyes and said, "Father, I thank you that you have heard me. ⁴²I knew that you always hear me, but I said this on account of the people standing around, that they may believe that you sent me." ⁴³When he had said these things, he cried out with a loud voice, "Lazarus, come out." ⁴⁴The man who had died came out, his hands and feet bound with

Lazarus and Jesus

>>DEATH STRIKES OUT

When death shows up, it smacks you in the face.

The news hit Rachelle like a lightning bolt. The principal's voice came through the speaker delivering the terrible news. Ashley, a classmate in her grade, was killed the night before when the car driven by her brother was struck by a drunk driver. Yesterday, she had seen Ashley by her locker. Today she was gone—forever.

Rachelle couldn't stop herself from crying. Her classmates sat motionless and silent. Why Ashley? Why now? How could God let this happen?

When death hits your school or a family you know, your faith in God gets tested big-time. Disbelief, denial, anger, and despair fill your thoughts and emotions. You feel numb and empty.

In these dark moments, you are not alone. When you feel overwhelmed by grief and fear, Jesus is there. If you've trusted Him with your life, your story is connected to Him. You know, Jesus cried, too. The Bible says that when Jesus' good friend Lazarus died, Jesus wept. When Lazarus's sisters, Mary and Martha, talked to Jesus, they were frustrated with Him. They had hoped that before their brother died, Jesus would get to their house and heal him. But Jesus had stayed where He was and didn't arrive until after Lazarus had died.

Do *you* believe in Jesus?

To learn how you can connect with Jesus *now,* turn to "Prayer: Getting Started in a Lifelong Relationship with Jesus Christ" on p. 97.

This was a crisis moment in their faith. Jesus told these sisters that their brother's death was not the end. He made a momentous claim, "I am the resurrection and the life," and a powerful promise, "Whoever believes in me, though he die, yet shall he live, and everyone who lives and believes in me shall never die." Then came the question to the sisters: "Do you believe this?"

Do you believe that Jesus is the resurrection and the life? Ask yourself:

>> Is Jesus really alive? Did He rise from the dead?

>> On this crucial point, how is Christianity distinctly different from all other religions?

>> Does knowing Jesus give you confidence and strength when death strikes someone close to you?

Jesus showed Mary and Martha a spectacular unexpected miracle. He called Lazarus out of his tomb and brought him back to life. He did this to show Mary, Martha, and the whole town that there is life after death. They saw that Jesus was more powerful than death. Lazarus didn't live forever; he died again years later. On that miracle day, however, people saw clear evidence that everyone who believes and trusts in Jesus can come to life again.

When death and tragedy strike, doorways of opportunity open. People who have been too busy for God stop and ask big questions about life. God uses these circumstances as painful doorways to help people connect to Him. Because of your faith in Christ you can show God's love to others in personal and practical ways. Here are some ways to respond to friends who are grieving:

>> Show up and support the family during the funeral activities and services. You will feel uncomfortable at times, but being there shows love and support.

>> Don't try to answer the difficult questions. It's better to listen with a caring spirit to the heartaches of friends and family. Just sitting with them helps.

>> We never understand God's timing and plan. Assure them God knows and cares, like Jesus did with Mary and Martha.

>> Don't preach sermons; instead, serve and help in practical ways.

>> Pray for the friends and family.

>> When the time is right (with God's help), explain the hope that Jesus gives you.

Let God build your faith and confidence in Him as you help others. Someday death will smack you in the face. Strengthen your connection to God now so you will be prepared.

linen strips, and his face wrapped with a cloth. Jesus said to them, "Unbind him, and let him go."

The Plot to Kill Jesus

[45]Many of the Jews therefore, who had come with Mary and had seen what he did, believed in him, [46]but some of them went to the Pharisees and told them what Jesus had done. [47]So the chief priests and the Pharisees gathered the Council and said, "What are we to do? For this man performs many signs. [48]If we let him go on like this, everyone will believe in him, and the Romans will come and take away both our place and our nation." [49]But one of them, Caiaphas, who was high priest that year, said to them, "You know nothing at all. [50]Nor do you understand that it is better for you that one man should die for the people, not that the whole nation should perish." [51]He did not say this of his own accord, but being high priest that year he prophesied that Jesus would die for the nation, [52]and not for the nation only, but also to gather into one the children of God who are scattered abroad. [53]So from that day on they made plans to put him to death.

[54]Jesus therefore no longer walked openly among the Jews, but went from there to the region near the wilderness, to a town called Ephraim, and there he stayed with the disciples.

[55]Now the Passover of the Jews was at hand, and many went up from the country to Jerusalem before the Passover to purify themselves. [56]They were looking for[1] Jesus and saying to one another as

1 Greek *were seeking for*

they stood in the temple, "What do you think? That he will not come to the feast at all?" ⁵⁷Now the chief priests and the Pharisees had given orders that if anyone knew where he was, he should let them know, so that they might arrest him.

Mary Anoints Jesus at Bethany

12 Six days before the Passover, Jesus therefore came to Bethany, where Lazarus was, whom Jesus had raised from the dead. ²So they gave a dinner for him there. Martha served, and Lazarus was one of those reclining with him at the table. ³Mary therefore took a pound[1] of expensive ointment made from pure nard, and anointed the feet of Jesus and wiped his feet with her hair. The house was filled with the fragrance of the perfume. ⁴But Judas Iscariot, one of his disciples (he who was about to betray him), said, ⁵"Why was this ointment not sold for three hundred denarii[2] and given to the poor?" ⁶He said this, not because he cared about the poor, but because he was a thief, and having charge of the moneybag he used to help himself to what was put into it. ⁷Jesus said, "Leave her alone, so that she may keep it[3] for the day of my burial. ⁸The poor you always have with you, but you do not always have me."

The Plot to Kill Lazarus

⁹When the large crowd of the Jews learned that Jesus[4] was there, they came, not only on account of him but also to see Lazarus, whom

1 Greek *litra*; a *litra* (or Roman pound) was equal to about 11 1/2 ounces or 327 grams   2 A *denarius* was a day's wage for a laborer   3 Or *Leave her alone; she intended to keep it*   4 Greek *he*

Mary Anoints Jesus' Feet

>>POUR OUT YOUR LOVE

What does true love look like? How do you know it's real? Here's a clue.

One night Jesus was eating dinner with Mary and Martha and Lazarus. After dinner, Mary broke open a jar of extremely expensive perfume and poured it over Jesus' feet. (Today, this might be comparable in price to treating Jesus to the most expensive luxury spa package or buying box seats for a World Series game.) Mary and her family weren't wealthy. This sealed jar of perfume was probably Mary's most valuable possession. She didn't open it, sprinkle a few drops, and give Jesus a quick foot massage. No, she broke the seal, poured every drop on Jesus' feet, and dried them with her hair. It shocked everyone! Judas, the disciple who would betray Jesus later that week, said it was a waste. He exclaimed, "The perfume could have been sold and the money given to the poor!"

Was it a waste of expensive perfume? Jesus had raised Mary's brother Lazarus from the dead! She wanted to say thank you and let Jesus know that she loved Him more than anything in the world. Mary lavishly expressed her love for Jesus. Cost was no issue.

How do you show Jesus you love Him?

Think like Mary. Focus on what Jesus has done for you—He gave His life to purchase forgiveness for your sin and to restore you to a relationship with God. Focus on what He is doing now—He loves you unconditionally, even when you mess up. Nobody loves you like Jesus. Nobody.

An authentic Christian lifestyle is anchored in this remarkable love. You have every reason to overflow with love and gratitude. People may wonder why you are so happy and so willing to give and help others. It comes from the never-ending love of Jesus flowing through you.

Abiding in Jesus empowers you to love and give generously as Mary did. You can give without loving, but you can't love without giving. This is not about money. There is no set price to pay or specific gift you must give. You don't do this to win God's approval or to gain some immediate reward. Authentic Christian living isn't about pleasing ourselves first and giving the leftovers to God and others. We respond to God's love by giving our best.

When we give to others, Jesus said it is like we are giving to Him.

>> Think about people in your life who need to see that God's love is real.

>> Consider what God has given you to share with others.

>> Crack open something valuable and precious to you. Give it away to someone in need.

>> Don't give to impress others.

>> Remember: Love = Giving. Giving shows that love is real.

he had raised from the dead. **10**So the chief priests made plans to put Lazarus to death as well, **11**because on account of him many of the Jews were going away and believing in Jesus.

The Triumphal Entry

12The next day *a*the large crowd that had come to the feast heard that Jesus was coming to Jerusalem. **13**So they took branches of palm trees and went out to meet him, crying out, "Hosanna! Blessed is he who comes in the name of the Lord, even the King of Israel!" **14**And Jesus found a young donkey and sat on it, just as it is written,

15 *b*"Fear not, daughter of Zion;
  behold, your king is coming,
    sitting on a donkey's colt!"

16His disciples did not understand these things at first, but when Jesus was glorified, then they remembered that these things had been written about him and had been done to him. **17**The crowd that had been with him when he called Lazarus out of the tomb and raised him from the dead continued to bear witness. **18**The reason why the crowd went to meet him was that they heard he had done this sign. **19**So the Pharisees said to one another, "You see that you are gaining nothing. Look, the world has gone after him."

Some Greeks Seek Jesus

[20]Now among those who went up to worship at the feast were some Greeks. [21]So these came to Philip, who was from Bethsaida in Galilee, and asked him, "Sir, we wish to see Jesus." [22]Philip went and told Andrew; Andrew and Philip went and told Jesus. [23]And Jesus answered them, "The hour has come for the Son of Man to be glorified. [24]Truly, truly, I say to you, unless a grain of wheat falls into the earth and dies, it remains alone; but if it dies, it bears much fruit. [25]Whoever loves his life loses it, and whoever hates his life in this world will keep it for eternal life. [26]If anyone serves me, he must follow me; and where I am, there will my servant be also. If anyone serves me, the Father will honor him.

The Son of Man Must Be Lifted Up

[27]"Now is my soul troubled. And what shall I say? 'Father, save me from this hour'? But for this purpose I have come to this hour. [28]Father, glorify your name." Then a voice came from heaven: "I have glorified it, and I will glorify it again." [29]The crowd that stood there and heard it said that it had thundered. Others said, "An angel has spoken to him." [30]Jesus answered, "This voice has come for your sake, not mine. [31]Now is the judgment of this world; now will the ruler of this world be cast out. [32]And I, when I am lifted up from the earth, will draw all people to myself." [33]He said this to show by what

kind of death he was going to die. ³⁴So the crowd answered him, "We have heard from the Law that the Christ remains forever. How can you say that the Son of Man must be lifted up? Who is this Son of Man?" ³⁵So Jesus said to them, "The light is among you for a little while longer. Walk while you have the light, lest darkness overtake you. The one who walks in the darkness does not know where he is going. ³⁶While you have the light, believe in the light, that you may become sons of light."

The Unbelief of the People

When Jesus had said these things, he departed and hid himself from them. ³⁷Though he had done so many signs before them, they still did not believe in him, ³⁸so that the word spoken by the prophet Isaiah might be fulfilled:

> ^c"Lord, who has believed what he heard from us,
>   and to whom has the arm of the Lord been revealed?"

³⁹Therefore they could not believe. For again Isaiah said,

> ⁴⁰   ^d"He has blinded their eyes
>   and hardened their heart,
>   lest they see with their eyes,
>   and understand with their heart, and turn,
>   and I would heal them."

c Isa. 53:1   d Isa. 6:10

⁴¹Isaiah said these things because he saw his glory and spoke of him. ⁴²Nevertheless, many even of the authorities believed in him, but for fear of the Pharisees they did not confess it, so that they would not be put out of the synagogue; ⁴³for they loved the glory that comes from man more than the glory that comes from God.

Jesus Came to Save the World

⁴⁴And Jesus cried out and said, "Whoever believes in me, believes not in me but in him who sent me. ⁴⁵And whoever sees me sees him who sent me. ⁴⁶I have come into the world as light, so that whoever believes in me may not remain in darkness. ⁴⁷If anyone hears my words and does not keep them, I do not judge him; for I did not come to judge the world but to save the world. ⁴⁸The one who rejects me and does not receive my words has a judge; the word that I have spoken will judge him on the last day. ⁴⁹For I have not spoken on my own authority, but the Father who sent me has himself given me a commandment—what to say and what to speak. ⁵⁰And I know that his commandment is eternal life. What I say, therefore, I say as the Father has told me."

Jesus Washes the Disciples' Feet

13 Now before the Feast of the Passover, when Jesus knew that his hour had come to depart out of this world to the Father, having loved his own who were in the world, he loved them to the end. ²During supper, when the devil had already put it into the heart of Judas Iscariot, Simon's son, to betray him, [3]Jesus, knowing that the Father had given all things into his hands, and that he had come from God and was going back to God, [4]rose from supper. He laid aside his outer garments, and taking a towel, tied it around his waist. [5]Then he poured water into a basin and began to wash the disciples' feet and to wipe them with the towel that was wrapped around him. [6]He came to Simon Peter, who said to him, "Lord, do you wash my feet?" [7]Jesus answered him, "What I am doing you do not understand now, but afterward you will understand." [8]Peter said to him, "You shall never wash my feet." Jesus answered him, "If I do not wash you, you have no share with me." [9]Simon Peter said to him, "Lord, not my feet only but also my hands and my head!" [10]Jesus said to him, "The one who has bathed does not need to wash, except for his feet,[1] but is completely clean. And you[2] are clean, but not every one of you." [11]For he knew who was to betray him; that was why he said, "Not all of you are clean."

[12]When he had washed their feet and put on his outer garments and resumed his place, he said to them, "Do you understand what I have done to you? [13]You call me Teacher and Lord, and you are right, for so I am. [14]If I then, your Lord and Teacher, have washed your feet, you also ought to wash one another's feet. [15]For I have given you an example, that you also should do just as I have done to you. [16]Truly, truly, I say to you, a servant[3] is not greater than his master, nor is a messenger greater than the one who sent him. [17]If you know these things, blessed are you if

---

1 Some manuscripts omit *except for his feet*   2 The Greek words for *you* in this verse are plural   3 Greek *bondservant*

you do them. [18]I am not speaking of all of you; I know whom I have chosen. But the Scripture will be fulfilled,[1] *a*'He who ate my bread has lifted his heel against me.' [19]I am telling you this now, before it takes place, that when it does take place you may believe that I am he. [20]Truly, truly, I say to you, whoever receives the one I send receives me, and whoever receives me receives the one who sent me."

One of You Will Betray Me

[21]After saying these things, Jesus was troubled in his spirit, and testified, "Truly, truly, I say to you, one of you will betray me." [22]The disciples looked at one another, uncertain of whom he spoke. [23]One of his disciples, whom Jesus loved, was reclining at table close to Jesus,[2] [24]so Simon Peter motioned to him to ask Jesus[3] of whom he was speaking. [25]So that disciple, leaning back against Jesus, said to him, "Lord, who is it?" [26]Jesus answered, "It is he to whom I will give this morsel of bread when I have dipped it." So when he had dipped the morsel, he gave it to Judas, the son of Simon Iscariot. [27]Then after he had taken the morsel, Satan entered into him. Jesus said to him, "What you are going to do, do quickly." [28]Now no one at the table knew why he said this to him. [29]Some thought that, because Judas had the moneybag, Jesus was telling him, "Buy what we need for the feast," or that he should give something to the poor. [30]So, after receiving the morsel of bread, he immediately went out. And it was night.

1 Greek *But in order that the Scripture may be fulfilled*   2 Greek *in the bosom of Jesus*   3 Greek lacks *Jesus*
a Ps. 41:9

A New Commandment

[31] When he had gone out, Jesus said, "Now is the Son of Man glorified, and God is glorified in him. [32] If God is glorified in him, God will also glorify him in himself, and glorify him at once. [33] Little children, yet a little while I am with you. You will seek me, and just as I said to the Jews, so now I also say to you, 'Where I am going you cannot come.' [34] A new commandment I give to you, that you love one another: just as I have loved you, you also are to love one another. [35] By this all people will know that you are my disciples, if you have love for one another."

Jesus Foretells Peter's Denial

[36] Simon Peter said to him, "Lord, where are you going?" Jesus answered him, "Where I am going you cannot follow me now, but you will follow afterward." [37] Peter said to him, "Lord, why can I not follow you now? I will lay down my life for you." [38] Jesus answered, "Will you lay down your life for me? Truly, truly, I say to you, the rooster will not crow till you have denied me three times.

I Am the Way, and the Truth, and the Life

14 "Let not your hearts be troubled. Believe in God;[1] believe also in me. [2] In my Father's house are many rooms. If it were not so, would I have told you that I go

1 Or *You believe in God*

to prepare a place for you? ³And if I go and prepare a place for you, I will come again and will take you to myself, that where I am you may be also. ⁴And you know the way to where I am going."[1] ⁵Thomas said to him, "Lord, we do not know where you are going. How can we know the way?" ⁶Jesus said to him, "I am the way, and the truth, and the life. No one comes to the Father except through me. ⁷If you had known me, you would have known my Father also.[2] From now on you do know him and have seen him."

⁸Philip said to him, "Lord, show us the Father, and it is enough for us." ⁹Jesus said to him, "Have I been with you so long, and you still do not know me, Philip? Whoever has seen me has seen the Father. How can you say, 'Show us the Father'? ¹⁰Do you not believe that I am in the Father and the Father is in me? The words that I say to you I do not speak on my own authority, but the Father who dwells in me does his works. ¹¹Believe me that I am in the Father and the Father is in me, or else believe on account of the works themselves.

¹²"Truly, truly, I say to you, whoever believes in me will also do the works that I do; and greater works than these will he do, because I am going to the Father. ¹³Whatever you ask in my name, this I will do, that the Father may be glorified in the Son. ¹⁴If you ask me[3] anything in my name, I will do it.

Jesus Promises the Holy Spirit

¹⁵"If you love me, you will keep my commandments. ¹⁶And I will ask the Father, and he will give you another Helper,[4] to be with you

---

1 Some manuscripts *Where I am going you know, and the way you know*   2 Or *If you know me, you will know my Father also*, or *If you have known me, you will know my Father also*   3 Some manuscripts omit *me*   4 Or *Advocate*, or *Counselor*; also 14:26; 15:26; 16:7

forever, ¹⁷ even the Spirit of truth, whom the world cannot receive, because it neither sees him nor knows him. You know him, for he dwells with you and will be in you.

¹⁸"I will not leave you as orphans; I will come to you. ¹⁹ Yet a little while and the world will see me no more, but you will see me. Because I live, you also will live. ²⁰ In that day you will know that I am in my Father, and you in me, and I in you. ²¹ Whoever has my commandments and keeps them, he it is who loves me. And he who loves me will be loved by my Father, and I will love him and manifest myself to him." ²² Judas (not Iscariot) said to him, "Lord, how is it that you will manifest yourself to us, and not to the world?" ²³ Jesus answered him, "If anyone loves me, he will keep my word, and my Father will love him, and we will come to him and make our home with him. ²⁴ Whoever does not love me does not keep my words. And the word that you hear is not mine but the Father's who sent me.

²⁵"These things I have spoken to you while I am still with you. ²⁶ But the Helper, the Holy Spirit, whom the Father will send in my name, he will teach you all things and bring to your remembrance all that I have said to you. ²⁷ Peace I leave with you; my peace I give to you. Not as the world gives do I give to you. Let not your hearts be troubled, neither let them be afraid. ²⁸ You heard me say to you, 'I am going away, and I will come to you.' If you loved me, you would have rejoiced, because I am going to the Father, for the Father is greater than I. ²⁹ And now I have told you before it takes place, so that when it does take place you may believe. ³⁰ I will no longer talk much with you, for the ruler of this world is coming. He has no claim on me,

³¹but I do as the Father has commanded me, so that the world may know that I love the Father. Rise, let us go from here.

I Am the True Vine

15 "I am the true vine, and my Father is the vinedresser. ²Every branch of mine that does not bear fruit he takes away, and every branch that does bear fruit he prunes, that it may bear more fruit. ³Already you are clean because of the word that I have spoken to you. ⁴Abide in me, and I in you. As the branch cannot bear fruit by itself, unless it abides in the vine, neither can you, unless you abide in me. ⁵I am the vine; you are the branches. Whoever abides in me and I in him, he it is that bears much fruit, for apart from me you can do nothing. ⁶If anyone does not abide in me he is thrown away like a branch and withers; and the branches are gathered, thrown into the fire, and burned. ⁷If you abide in me, and my words abide in you, ask whatever you wish, and it will be done for you. ⁸By this my Father is glorified, that you bear much fruit and so prove to be my disciples. ⁹As the Father has loved me, so have I loved you. Abide in my love. ¹⁰If you keep my commandments, you will abide in love, just as I have kept my Father's commandments and abide in his love. ¹¹These things I have spoken to you, that my joy may be in you, and that your joy may be full.

¹²"This is my commandment, that you love one another as I have loved you. ¹³Greater love has no one than this, that someone lays down his life for his friends. ¹⁴You are my friends if you do what

I command you. [15] No longer do I call you servants,[1] for the servant[2] does not know what his master is doing; but I have called you friends, for all that I have heard from my Father I have made known to you. [16] You did not choose me, but I chose you and appointed you that you should go and bear fruit and that your fruit should abide, so that whatever you ask the Father in my name, he may give it to you. [17] These things I command you, so that you will love one another.

The Hatred of the World

[18] "If the world hates you, know that it has hated me before it hated you. [19] If you were of the world, the world would love you as its own; but because you are not of the world, but I chose you out of the world, therefore the world hates you. [20] Remember the word that I said to you: 'A servant is not greater than his master.' If they persecuted me, they will also persecute you. If they kept my word, they will also keep yours. [21] But all these things they will do to you on account of my name, because they do not know him who sent me. [22] If I had not come and spoken to them, they would not have been guilty of sin,[3] but now they have no excuse for their sin. [23] Whoever hates me hates my Father also. [24] If I had not done among them the works that no one else did, they would not be guilty of sin, but now they have seen and hated both me and my Father. [25] But the word that is written in their Law must be fulfilled: a 'They hated me without a cause.'

[26] "But when the Helper comes, whom I will send to you from the Father, the Spirit of truth, who proceeds from the Father, he will bear

---

1 Greek *bondservants* 2 Greek *bondservant*; also verse 20 3 Greek *they would not have sin*; also verse 24
a Ps. 35:19, or 69:4

witness about me. ²⁷And you also will bear witness, because you have been with me from the beginning.

16 "I have said all these things to you to keep you from falling away. ²They will put you out of the synagogues. Indeed, the hour is coming when whoever kills you will think he is offering service to God. ³And they will do these things because they have not known the Father, nor me. ⁴But I have said these things to you, that when their hour comes you may remember that I told them to you.

The Work of the Holy Spirit

"I did not say these things to you from the beginning, because I was with you. ⁵But now I am going to him who sent me, and none of you asks me, 'Where are you going?' ⁶But because I have said these things to you, sorrow has filled your heart. ⁷Nevertheless, I tell you the truth: it is to your advantage that I go away, for if I do not go away, the Helper will not come to you. But if I go, I will send him to you. ⁸And when he comes, he will convict the world concerning sin and righteousness and judgment: ⁹concerning sin, because they do not believe in me; ¹⁰concerning righteousness, because I go to the Father, and you will see me no longer; ¹¹concerning judgment, because the ruler of this world is judged.

¹²"I still have many things to say to you, but you cannot bear them now. ¹³When the Spirit of truth comes, he will guide you into all the truth, for he will not speak on his own authority, but whatever he hears he will speak, and he will declare to you the things that are to

WHAT IS "ABIDING"?

You don't want to miss this!
In John 15:1-17, Jesus invites us to *abide* in Him. Notice how many times the word *abide* appears there—eleven times! Other ways of expressing this idea are "to connect, to be close, to be attached." *Abiding* means to remain with someone, to live so connected to someone else that their life provides the life-giving nourishment needed for one's own existence.

For Christians, to abide in Christ is to dwell with Him and make our home in Him. Jesus wants us to be intimately connected to Him every day so that My Story intersects with His story moment by moment. The most important dynamic in our lives as followers of Jesus Christ is our abiding relationship with Him. When we abide in Him and stay near Him daily, we will be able to bear lasting fruit for His kingdom.

Think about this.
One way to abide in Christ is to involve Him in every part of our lives. This means we saturate ourselves with God and His Word. God wants us to soak up His Word like a sponge. Invite Christ into every aspect of our lives. My Story can be changed by God's Story on a daily basis as I soak every detail of my life in Him and His Spirit. Abiding is the beginning, the middle, and the end of 3Story living.

It's all about overlapping, intersecting stories.
The more that God's Story overlaps with My Story, the more prepared I am to make appropriate connections with other people (with Their Story). Conversely, the less connected to Jesus I find myself, the less prepared I am to faithfully engage in the 3Story process.

While God's Story is life-changing, what we really want to do is break through the *story* of Jesus Christ and actually meet the *Person* of Jesus Christ. Jesus Himself, not just His story, brings change.

"Apart from me you can do nothing." That's what Jesus said.
Take another look at John 15. We are reminded that the branches have one job—to stay connected to the vine. It is not for us to worry about producing the fruit. Our job is to stay intimately connected to the Vine.

We cannot earn more of Christ's love by abiding; He loves us no matter what. But as we allow His Spirit to draw us closer to Him, we will be more open to Christ's hold on our hearts.

He can't take His eyes off you!

Jesus is devoted to you. It's as though He can't take His eyes off you. To abide in Jesus is to be devoted to Him, to be unable to take your eyes off Him. Abiding is the most important part of effectively living a 3Story life. Abiding is the first important story connection we make in order to confidently, effectively share God's Story with our friends.

You might wonder . . .

How do I get started?

It is a combination of *hanging out* with Jesus and *text messaging* with Him along the way. You can begin by talking to Jesus a little at a time, sort of like short text messages. Then take a few minutes and read a short portion of this book, the Gospel of John. Then wait. Listen for God's voice. At first it might feel a little weird. But give it a try. He speaks to us through His Word. He will help you to hear His voice.

How do I know when I'm actually abiding?

Great question! Abiding can feel like a great big mystery. You'll know you are abiding when you start feeling and seeing changes in the way you treat people at the lunch table, in class, at home. You'll begin to want to do the right thing. You won't be perfect, but you will see things begin to change. You may also find that you actually want to hear from Jesus more often.

How do I begin abiding again when I mess up?

We all mess up at times, and starting over can be a challenge. No worries! Jesus Christ is full of second chances! He will help you begin abiding in Him again. All you have to do is ask. Then start obeying Him immediately. Start talking to Him right away. Start listening again. Use this book to help you. You only need to read a little at a time. Don't choke on the Word of God; rather, read it slowly, asking Jesus to speak to your specific situation. He will!

69

come. ¹⁴He will glorify me, for he will take what is mine and declare it to you. ¹⁵All that the Father has is mine; therefore I said that he will take what is mine and declare it to you.

Your Sorrow Will Turn into Joy

¹⁶"A little while, and you will see me no longer; and again a little while, and you will see me." ¹⁷So some of his disciples said to one another, "What is this that he says to us, 'A little while, and you will not see me, and again a little while, and you will see me'; and, 'because I am going to the Father?'" ¹⁸So they were saying, "What does he mean by 'a little while'? We do not know what he is talking about." ¹⁹Jesus knew that they wanted to ask him, so he said to them, "Is this what you are asking yourselves, what I meant by saying, 'A little while and you will not see me, and again a little while and you will see me'? ²⁰Truly, truly, I say to you, you will weep and lament, but the world will rejoice. You will be sorrowful, but your sorrow will turn into joy. ²¹When a woman is giving birth, she has sorrow because her hour has come, but when she has delivered the baby, she no longer remembers the anguish, for joy that a human being has been born into the world. ²²So also you have sorrow now, but I will see you again and your hearts will rejoice, and no one will take your joy from you. ²³In that day you will ask nothing of me. Truly, truly, I say to you, whatever you ask of the Father in my name, he will give it to you. ²⁴Until now you have asked nothing in my name. Ask, and you will receive, that your joy may be full.

I Have Overcome the World

[25]"I have said these things to you in figures of speech. The hour is coming when I will no longer speak to you in figures of speech but will tell you plainly about the Father. [26]In that day you will ask in my name, and I do not say to you that I will ask the Father on your behalf; [27]for the Father himself loves you, because you have loved me and have believed that I came from God.[1] [28]I came from the Father and have come into the world, and now I am leaving the world and going to the Father."

[29]His disciples said, "Ah, now you are speaking plainly and not using figurative speech! [30]Now we know that you know all things and do not need anyone to question you; this is why we believe that you came from God." [31]Jesus answered them, "Do you now believe? [32]Behold, the hour is coming, indeed it has come, when you will be scattered, each to his own home, and will leave me alone. Yet I am not alone, for the Father is with me. [33]I have said these things to you, that in me you may have peace. In the world you will have tribulation. But take heart; I have overcome the world."

The High Priestly Prayer

17 When Jesus had spoken these words, he lifted up his eyes to heaven, and said, "Father, the hour has come; glorify your Son that the Son may glorify you, [2]since

---

1 Some manuscripts *from the Father*

you have given him authority over all flesh, to give eternal life to all whom you have given him. ³And this is eternal life, that they know you the only true God, and Jesus Christ whom you have sent. ⁴I glorified you on earth, having accomplished the work that you gave me to do. ⁵And now, Father, glorify me in your own presence with the glory that I had with you before the world existed.

⁶"I have manifested your name to the people whom you gave me out of the world. Yours they were, and you gave them to me, and they have kept your word. ⁷Now they know that everything that you have given me is from you. ⁸For I have given them the words that you gave me, and they have received them and have come to know in truth that I came from you; and they have believed that you sent me. ⁹I am praying for them. I am not praying for the world but for those whom you have given me, for they are yours. ¹⁰All mine are yours, and yours are mine, and I am glorified in them. ¹¹And I am no longer in the world, but they are in the world, and I am coming to you. Holy Father, keep them in your name, which you have given me, that they may be one, even as we are one. ¹²While I was with them, I kept them in your name, which you have given me. I have guarded them, and not one of them has been lost except the son of destruction, that the Scripture might be fulfilled. ¹³But now I am coming to you, and these things I speak in the world, that they may have my joy fulfilled in themselves. ¹⁴I have given them your word, and the world has hated them because they are not of the world, just as I am not of the world. ¹⁵I do not ask that you take them out of the world, but that you keep them from the evil one.[1] ¹⁶They are not of the world, just as I am not of the world.

1 Or *from evil*

[17]Sanctify them[1] in the truth; your word is truth. [18]As you sent me into the world, so I have sent them into the world. [19]And for their sake I consecrate myself,[2] that they also may be sanctified[3] in truth.

[20]"I do not ask for these only, but also for those who will believe in me through their word, [21]that they may all be one, just as you, Father, are in me, and I in you, that they also may be in us, so that the world may believe that you have sent me. [22]The glory that you have given me I have given to them, that they may be one even as we are one, [23]I in them and you in me, that they may become perfectly one, so that the world may know that you sent me and loved them even as you loved me. [24]Father, I desire that they also, whom you have given me, may be with me where I am, to see my glory that you have given me because you loved me before the foundation of the world. [25]O righteous Father, even though the world does not know you, I know you, and these know that you have sent me. [26]I made known to them your name, and I will continue to make it known, that the love with which you have loved me may be in them, and I in them."

Betrayal and Arrest of Jesus

18 When Jesus had spoken these words, he went out with his disciples across the Kidron Valley, where there was a garden, which he and his disciples entered. [2]Now Judas, who betrayed him, also knew the place, for Jesus often met there with his disciples. [3][a] So Judas, having procured a band of soldiers and some officers from the chief priests and the Pharisees, went there

1 Greek *Set them apart* (for holy service to God)   2 Greek *I set myself apart* (for holy service to God); or *I sanctify myself*   3 Greek *may be set apart* (for holy service to God)   a For 18:3-11 see parallels Matt. 26:47-56; Mark 14:43-50; Luke 22:47-53

with lanterns and torches and weapons. [4] Then Jesus, knowing all that would happen to him, came forward and said to them, "Whom do you seek?" [5] They answered him, "Jesus of Nazareth." Jesus said to them, "I am he." [1] Judas, who betrayed him, was standing with them. [6] When Jesus [2] said to them, "I am he," they drew back and fell to the ground. [7] So he asked them again, "Whom do you seek?" And they said, "Jesus of Nazareth." [8] Jesus answered, "I told you that I am he. So, if you seek me, let these men go." [9] This was to fulfill the word that he had spoken: "Of those whom you gave me I have lost not one." [10] Then Simon Peter, having a sword, drew it and struck the high priest's servant [3] and cut off his right ear. (The servant's name was Malchus.) [11] So Jesus said to Peter, "Put your sword into its sheath; shall I not drink the cup that the Father has given me?"

Jesus Before the High Priest

[12] So the band of soldiers and their captain and the officers of the Jews arrested Jesus and bound him. [13] First they led him to Annas, for he was the father-in-law of Caiaphas, who was high priest that year. [14] It was Caiaphas who had advised the Jews that it would be expedient that one man should die for the people.

Peter Denies Jesus

[15] Simon Peter followed Jesus, and so did another disciple. Since that disciple was known to the high priest, he entered with Jesus into

---

1 Greek *I am*; also verses 6, 8   2 Greek *he*   3 Greek *bondservant*; twice in this verse

the court of the high priest, [16]*a* but Peter stood outside at the door. So the other disciple, who was known to the high priest, went out and spoke to the servant girl who kept watch at the door, and brought Peter in. [17] The servant girl at the door said to Peter, "You also are not one of this man's disciples, are you?" He said, "I am not." [18] Now the servants[1] and officers had made a charcoal fire, because it was cold, and they were standing and warming themselves. Peter also was with them, standing and warming himself.

The High Priest Questions Jesus

[19] The high priest then questioned Jesus about his disciples and his teaching. [20] Jesus answered him, "I have spoken openly to the world. I have always taught in synagogues and in the temple, where all Jews come together. I have said nothing in secret. [21] Why do you ask me? Ask those who have heard me what I said to them; they know what I said." [22] When he had said these things, one of the officers standing by struck Jesus with his hand, saying, "Is that how you answer the high priest?" [23] Jesus answered him, "If what I said is wrong, bear witness about the wrong; but if what I said is right, why do you strike me?" [24] Annas then sent him bound to Caiaphas the high priest.

Peter Denies Jesus Again

[25]*b* Now Simon Peter was standing and warming himself. So they said to him, "You also are not one of his disciples, are you?"

---

1 Greek *bondservants*; also verse 26   a For 18:16-18 see parallels Matt. 26:69, 70; Mark 14:66-68; Luke 22:55-57
b For 18:25-27 see parallels Matt. 26:71-75; Mark 14:69-72; Luke 22:58-62

He denied it and said, "I am not." ²⁶One of the servants of the high priest, a relative of the man whose ear Peter had cut off, asked, "Did I not see you in the garden with him?" ²⁷Peter again denied it, and at once a rooster crowed.

Jesus Before Pilate

²⁸Then they led Jesus from the house of Caiaphas to the governor's headquarters.[1] It was early morning. They themselves did not enter the governor's headquarters, so that they would not be defiled, but could eat the Passover. ²⁹ ᵃSo Pilate went outside to them and said, "What accusation do you bring against this man?" ³⁰They answered him, "If this man were not doing evil, we would not have delivered him over to you." ³¹Pilate said to them, "Take him yourselves and judge him by your own law." The Jews said to him, "It is not lawful for us to put anyone to death." ³²This was to fulfill the word that Jesus had spoken to show by what kind of death he was going to die.

My Kingdom Is Not of This World

³³So Pilate entered his headquarters again and called Jesus and said to him, "Are you the King of the Jews?" ³⁴Jesus answered, "Do you say this of your own accord, or did others say it to you about me?" ³⁵Pilate answered, "Am I a Jew? Your own nation and the chief priests have delivered you over to me. What have you done?" ³⁶Jesus

---

1 Greek *the praetorium*   a For 18:29-38 see parallels Matt. 27:11-14; Mark 15:1-5; Luke 23:1-3

answered, "My kingdom is not of this world. If my kingdom were of this world, my servants would have been fighting, that I might not be delivered over to the Jews. But my kingdom is not from the world." ³⁷ Then Pilate said to him, "So you are a king?" Jesus answered, "You say that I am a king. For this purpose I was born and for this purpose I have come into the world— to bear witness to the truth. Everyone who is of the truth listens to my voice." ³⁸ Pilate said to him, "What is truth?"

After he had said this, he went back outside to the Jews and told them, "I find no guilt in him. ³⁹ᵃ But you have a custom that I should release one man for you at the Passover. So do you want me to release to you the King of the Jews?" ⁴⁰ They cried out again, "Not this man, but Barabbas!" Now Barabbas was a robber.

Jesus Delivered to Be Crucified

19 Then Pilate took Jesus and flogged him. ² And the soldiers twisted together a crown of thorns and put it on his head and arrayed him in a purple robe. ³ They came up to him, saying, "Hail, King of the Jews!" and struck him with their hands. ⁴ Pilate went out again and said to them, "See, I am bringing him out to you that you may know that I find no guilt in him." ⁵ So Jesus came out, wearing the crown of thorns and the purple robe. Pilate said to them, "Behold the man!" ⁶ When the chief priests and the officers saw him, they cried out, "Crucify him, crucify him!" Pilate said to them, "Take him yourselves and crucify him,

a For 18:39, 40 see parallels Matt. 27:15-18, 20-23; Mark 15:6-14; Luke 23:18-23

for I find no guilt in him." [7]The Jews answered him, "We have a law, and according to that law he ought to die because he has made himself the Son of God." [8]When Pilate heard this statement, he was even more afraid. [9]He entered his headquarters again and said to Jesus, "Where are you from?" But Jesus gave him no answer. [10]So Pilate said to him, "You will not speak to me? Do you not know that I have authority to release you and authority to crucify you?" [11]Jesus answered him, "You would have no authority over me at all unless it had been given you from above. Therefore he who delivered me over to you has the greater sin."

[12]From then on Pilate sought to release him, but the Jews cried out, "If you release this man, you are not Caesar's friend. Everyone who makes himself a king opposes Caesar." [13]So when Pilate heard these words, he brought Jesus out and sat down on the judgment seat at a place called The Stone Pavement, and in Aramaic[1] Gabbatha. [14]Now it was the day of Preparation of the Passover. It was about the sixth hour.[2] He said to the Jews, "Behold your King!" [15]They cried out, "Away with him, away with him, crucify him!" Pilate said to them, "Shall I crucify your King?" The chief priests answered, "We have no king but Caesar." [16]So he delivered him over to them to be crucified.

The Crucifixion

So they took Jesus, [17]and he went out, bearing his own cross, to the place called the place of a skull, which in Aramaic is called

---

1 Or *Hebrew*; also verses 17, 20   2 That is, about noon

Golgotha. **18**There they crucified him, and with him two others, one on either side, and Jesus between them. **19**Pilate also wrote an inscription and put it on the cross. It read, "Jesus of Nazareth, the King of the Jews." **20**Many of the Jews read this inscription, for the place where Jesus was crucified was near the city, and it was written in Aramaic, in Latin, and in Greek. **21**So the chief priests of the Jews said to Pilate, "Do not write, 'The King of the Jews,' but rather, 'This man said, I am King of the Jews.'" **22**Pilate answered, "What I have written I have written."

23When the soldiers had crucified Jesus, they took his garments and divided them into four parts, one part for each soldier; also his tunic.[1] But the tunic was seamless, woven in one piece from top to bottom, **24**so they said to one another, "Let us not tear it, but cast lots for it to see whose it shall be." This was to fulfill the Scripture which says,

> *a*"They divided my garments among them,
>   and for my clothing they cast lots."

So the soldiers did these things, **25**but standing by the cross of Jesus were mother and his mother's sister, Mary the wife of Clopas, and Mary Magdalene. **26**When Jesus saw his mother and the disciple whom he loved standing nearby, he said to his mother, "Woman, behold, your son!" **27**Then he said to the disciple, "Behold, your mother!" And from that hour the disciple took her to his own home.

---

1 Greek *chiton*, a long garment worn under the cloak next to the skin   a Ps. 22:18

The Death of Jesus

28 After this, Jesus, knowing that all was now finished, said (to fulfill the Scripture), "I thirst." 29 A jar full of sour wine stood there, so they put a sponge full of the sour wine on a hyssop branch and held it to his mouth. 30 When Jesus had received the sour wine, he said, "It is finished," and he bowed his head and gave up his spirit.

Jesus' Side Is Pierced

31 Since it was the day of Preparation, and so that the bodies would not remain on the cross on the Sabbath (for that Sabbath was a high day), the Jews asked Pilate that their legs might be broken and that they might be taken away. 32 So the soldiers came and broke the legs of the first, and of the other who had been crucified with him. 33 But when they came to Jesus and saw that he was already dead, they did not break his legs. 34 But one of the soldiers pierced his side with a spear, and at once there came out blood and water. 35 He who saw it has borne witness— his testimony is true, and he knows that he is telling the truth— that you also may believe. 36 For these things took place that the Scripture might be fulfilled: a "Not one of his bones will be broken." 37 And again another Scripture says, b "They will look on him whom they have pierced."

a Ex. 12:46; Num. 9:12   b Zech. 12:10

Jesus Is Buried

³⁸*a* After these things Joseph of Arimathea, who was a disciple of Jesus, but secretly for fear of the Jews, asked Pilate that he might take away the body of Jesus, and Pilate gave him permission. So he came and took away his body. ³⁹Nicodemus also, who earlier had come to Jesus[1] by night, came bringing a mixture of myrrh and aloes, about seventy-five pounds[2] in weight. ⁴⁰So they took the body of Jesus and bound it in linen cloths with the spices, as is the burial custom of the Jews. ⁴¹Now in the place where he was crucified there was a garden, and in the garden a new tomb in which no one had yet been laid. ⁴²So because of the Jewish day of Preparation, since the tomb was close at hand, they laid Jesus there.

The Resurrection

20 Now on the first day of the week Mary Magdalene came to the tomb early, while it was still dark, and saw that the stone had been taken away from the tomb. ²So she ran and went to Simon Peter and the other disciple, the one whom Jesus loved, and said to them, "They have taken the Lord out of the tomb, and we do not know where they have laid him." ³So Peter went out with the other disciple, and they were going toward the tomb. ⁴Both of them were running together, but the other disciple outran Peter and reached the tomb first. ⁵And stooping to

1 Greek *him* 2 Greek *one hundred litras*; a *litra* (or Roman pound) was equal to about 11 1/2 ounces or 327 grams
a For 19:38–42 see parallels Matt. 27:57-61; Mark 15:42-47; Luke 23:50-56

look in, he saw the linen cloths lying there, but he did not go in. ⁶Then Simon Peter came, following him, and went into the tomb. He saw the linen cloths lying there, ⁷and the face cloth, which had been on Jesus'[1] head, not lying with the linen cloths but folded up in a place by itself. ⁸Then the other disciple, who had reached the tomb first, also went in, and he saw and believed; ⁹for as yet they did not understand the Scripture, that he must rise from the dead. ¹⁰Then the disciples went back to their homes.

Jesus Appears to Mary Magdalene

¹¹But Mary stood weeping outside the tomb, and as she wept she stooped to look into the tomb. ¹²And she saw two angels in white, sitting where the body of Jesus had lain, one at the head and one at the feet. ¹³They said to her, "Woman, why are you weeping?" She said to them, "They have taken away my Lord, and I do not know where they have laid him." ¹⁴Having said this, she turned around and saw Jesus standing, but she did not know that it was Jesus. ¹⁵Jesus said to her, "Woman, why are you weeping? Whom are you seeking?" Supposing him to be the gardener, she said to him, "Sir, if you have carried him away, tell me where you have laid him, and I will take him away." ¹⁶Jesus said to her, "Mary." She turned and said to him in Aramaic,[2] "Rabboni!" (which means Teacher). ¹⁷Jesus said to her, "Do not cling to me, for I have not yet ascended to the Father; but go to my brothers and say to them, 'I am ascending to my Father and your Father, to my God and your God.'" ¹⁸Mary Magdalene went

1 Greek *his* 2 Or *Hebrew*

and announced to the disciples, "I have seen the Lord"—and that he had said these things to her.

Jesus Appears to the Disciples

[19]On the evening of that day, the first day of the week, the doors being locked where the disciples were for fear of the Jews, Jesus came and stood among them and said to them, "Peace be with you." [20]When he had said this, he showed them his hands and his side. Then the disciples were glad when they saw the Lord. [21]Jesus said to them again, "Peace be with you. As the Father has sent me, even so I am sending you." [22]And when he had said this, he breathed on them and said to them, "Receive the Holy Spirit. [23]If you forgive the sins of anyone, they are forgiven; if you withhold forgiveness from anyone, it is withheld."

Jesus and Thomas

[24]Now Thomas, one of the Twelve, called the Twin,[1] was not with them when Jesus came. [25]So the other disciples told him, "We have seen the Lord." But he said to them, "Unless I see in his hands the mark of the nails, and place my finger into the mark of the nails, and place my hand into his side, I will never believe."

[26]Eight days later, his disciples were inside again, and Thomas was with them. Although the doors were locked, Jesus came and stood among them and said, "Peace be with you." [27]Then he said to Thomas, "Put your finger here, and see my hands; and put out

1 Greek *Didymus*

Thomas Has Questions

>>I DOUBT IT!

Most human beings operate out of a "show me" mentality. We want proof. We question everything. If we do not experience something firsthand or witness an event with our own eyes, we quickly respond with, "I doubt it." Thomas was like that. He simply wanted the facts.

In John chapter 14 we read that Jesus told the disciples He was going away to prepare a place for them. "And you know the way to where I am going," He said. None of the disciples had a clue where this place was, but only Thomas spoke up. He said, "Lord, we do not know where you are going. How can we know the way?" So let's not call him "Doubting Thomas" anymore. "Give-me-the-facts Thomas" would be more accurate.

Later, when the rest of the disciples reported to Thomas that they had seen the resurrected Jesus, the news was just too difficult to comprehend. It seemed unbelievable, and Thomas was honest enough to simply say, "I doubt it." So how did Jesus respond to Thomas's desire to see the evidence?

First, Jesus gave Thomas time to think. He waited a week before He showed up again! If we were in charge of the disciples, we'd probably lose sleep over Thomas's unbelief and his request for proof. We'd have already lost Judas; now, we seemed to be losing Thomas. We'd declare an emergency. But that's not how Jesus reacted. He wasn't threatened. He simply waited.

Then, at the right time, Jesus did show up—unmistakably and rather spectacularly! He offered the exact proof Thomas had asked for. Then He said, "Do not disbelieve, but believe." Seeing Jesus' wounds, seeing Him alive, got Thomas's attention! He simply replied, "My Lord and my God!"

Jesus is okay with our questions. He understands our doubts. Having doubts and fears shows that our minds are working. Romans 12:2 urges us to renew our minds: "Do not be conformed to this world, but be transformed by the renewal of your mind, that by testing you may discern what is the will of God, what is good and acceptable and perfect." We need to use our brains to understand our need for Jesus. The same is true for our friends as they learn about God's Story.

As you abide in Christ and strengthen the connection between God's Story and your story, look for ways to build your faith.

>> Keep reading the Bible.
>> Hang out with those who have a strong faith.
>> Get involved in a church where your faith is encouraged.
>> Find positive music, magazines, and movies.
>> Get to know the life of Jesus.

You don't have to have all the answers to believe God's Story. Thomas had the courage to be honest with his doubts. If you do the same, you can expect the same response from Jesus. Then you can pass on the same respect to your friends.

>> Jesus gives you time. Have the same patience with your friends.
>> Jesus will show up. Love your friends as you connect to their stories.
>> Jesus hears your doubts. Listen carefully to your friends' questions.

There will never be a better time than now for you to wholeheartedly follow Jesus and to reach out to your friends with God's love. No doubt about it!

your hand, and place it in my side. Do not disbelieve, but believe."
28Thomas answered him, "My Lord and my God!" 29Jesus said to him, "Have you believed because you have seen me? Blessed are those who have not seen and yet have believed."

The Purpose of This Book

30 Now Jesus did many other signs in the presence of the disciples, which are not written in this book; 31 but these are written so that you may believe that Jesus is the Christ, the Son of God, and that by believing you may have life in his name.

Jesus Appears to Seven Disciples

21 After this Jesus revealed himself again to the disciples by the Sea of Tiberias, and he revealed himself in this way. 2Simon Peter, Thomas (called the Twin), Nathanael of Cana in Galilee, the sons of Zebedee, and two others of his disciples were together. 3Simon Peter said to them, "I am going fishing." They said to him, "We will go with you." They went out and got into the boat, but that night they caught nothing.

4Just as day was breaking, Jesus stood on the shore; yet the disciples did not know that it was Jesus. 5Jesus said to them, "Children, do you have any fish?" They answered him, "No." 6He said to them, "Cast the net on the right side of the boat, and you will find some." So they cast it, and now they were not able to haul it in, because of the quantity of fish. [7]That disciple whom Jesus loved therefore said to Peter, "It is the Lord!" When Simon Peter heard that it was the Lord, he put on his outer garment, for he was stripped for work, and threw himself into the sea. [8]The other disciples came in the boat, dragging the net full of fish, for they were not far from the land, but about a hundred yards[1] off.

[9]When they got out on land, they saw a charcoal fire in place, with fish laid out on it, and bread. [10]Jesus said to them, "Bring some of the fish that you have just caught." [11]So Simon Peter went aboard and hauled the net ashore, full of large fish, 153 of them. And although there were so many, the net was not torn. [12]Jesus said to them, "Come and have breakfast." Now none of the disciples dared ask him, "Who are you?" They knew it was the Lord. [13]Jesus came and took the bread and gave it to them, and so with the fish. [14]This was now the third time that Jesus was revealed to the disciples after he was raised from the dead.

Jesus and Peter

[15]When they had finished breakfast, Jesus said to Simon Peter, "Simon, son of John, do you love me more than these?" He said to him, "Yes, Lord; you know that I love you." He said to him, "Feed my lambs." [16]He said to him a second time, "Simon, son of John, do you love me?" He said to him, "Yes, Lord; you know that I love you." He said to him, "Tend my sheep." [17]He said to him the third time, "Simon, son of John, do you love me?" Peter was grieved because

---

1 Greek *two hundred cubits*; a *cubit* was about 18 inches or 45 centimeters

Jesus and Peter

>>GOD HIRES FAILURES

What are some things that will get you fired from a job? (Check one or more.)

___ Argue with the boss.

___ Disagree with the boss's plan in front of the other workers.

___ Make big promises that you don't keep.

___ Do exactly what the boss told you *not* to do.

___ When the boss needs you most, don't show up.

___ All of the above.

Any of these actions would probably end up in job failure, right? And you could forget about being rehired.

Peter knew all about job failure as a disciple. He blew it big-time during the week Jesus was crucified. He argued about Jesus' washing his feet. He made a big, hardheaded speech about how people would have to kill *him* first before anyone would hurt Jesus. He started a foolhardy fight in the garden of Gethsemane when Jesus was arrested. Those soldiers would have cut him to pieces if Jesus hadn't stepped in. While Jesus was on trial, Peter snuck around the temple courtyards and denied that he even knew Him. It was exactly what Jesus had warned Peter would happen. Failure, big-time. Then Jesus was crucified, and it was all over.

Before he left Jerusalem, Peter had heard the big news. Some women were saying that Jesus' body was missing from His tomb. Mary said she had seen Jesus and had talked to Him. The thought of seeing Jesus again put a shiver up Peter's spine. After all his failures, how could he face Jesus?

Dejected, Peter went home to Galilee and went fishing. He and his buddies worked all night and caught nothing. Then they heard a familiar voice shouting from the shore, "Drop the net on the right side of the boat." When they did that, the fish filled the nets! Peter had seen Jesus perform this same miracle about three years earlier. He dove into the water and swam to shore. There stood Jesus, alive and ready to talk.

Jesus didn't say, "You stupid disciple" or "I told you so" or "You're fired!" He asked the only question that mattered—"Do you love me?" Jesus made it clear that He wanted Peter on His leadership team. Jesus hadn't given up on Peter. Jesus gave Peter a new job as a leader in His church that would explode in growth in the weeks to follow.

Peter had followed Jesus for three years, slowly connecting his story to God's Story. His failures revealed Peter as a man still full of himself, doing and saying what brought him attention rather than listening to and obeying Jesus. After talking with the risen Lord by the lake, Peter wasn't the same man. Gone was his big mouth, his hunger for approval from others, and his desire to be a big shot in God's kingdom. He had a new humility and forgiving spirit. If Jesus could forgive him, Peter could forgive and encourage others who would stumble and fail.

God often uses pressure and difficult circumstances as opportunities to strengthen our connection to Jesus and His story. It's a lifetime journey in which we're always learning and growing—sometimes from miserable failure and painful mistakes. But God is in the business of rehiring failures, and His love and grace never end.

Our failures can prepare us to engage honestly with other people and their stories in these ways:

>> We don't condemn them.

>> We're as patient and compassionate with them as Jesus is with us.

>> Our stories overflow and energize us.

>> We share with others the unconditional love and forgiveness we find in Jesus.

>> God never "fires" us when we fail.

>> We become living examples of His life-changing story.

he said to him the third time, "Do you love me?" and he said to him, "Lord, you know everything; you know that I love you." Jesus said to him, "Feed my sheep. [18]Truly, truly, I say to you, when you were young, you used to dress yourself and walk wherever you wanted, but when you are old, you will stretch out your hands, and another will dress you and carry you where you do not want to go." [19](This he said to show by what kind of death he was to glorify God.) And after saying this he said to him, "Follow me."

Jesus and the Beloved Apostle

[20]Peter turned and saw the disciple whom Jesus loved following them, the one who had been reclining at table close to him and had said, "Lord, who is it that is going to betray you?" [21]When Peter saw him, he said to Jesus, "Lord, what about this man?" [22]Jesus said to him, "If it is my will that he remain until I come, what is that to you? You follow me!" [23]So the saying spread abroad among the brothers[1] that this disciple was not to die; yet Jesus did not say to him that he was not to die, but, "If it is my will that he remain until I come, what is that to you?"

[24]This is the disciple who is bearing witness about these things, and who has written these things, and we know that his testimony is true.

[25]Now there are also many other things that Jesus did. Were every one of them to be written, I suppose that the world itself could not contain the books that would be written.

1 Or *brothers and sisters*

DEFINITIONS OF 3STORY
WORDS AND PHRASES

Abiding is best defined through the words of Jesus in John 15. To abide is to remain with Jesus, to endure, to live so closely with Him that His life provides the nourishment we need to survive day to day. It is the overlap between My Story and God's Story; He pursues relationship with us, and we respond to Him.

Being Real is best demonstrated by the authentic ways Jesus had relationships with people. Being real means we have fewer secrets. We pretend and act less. We admit our dreams, hopes, needs, and failures. We invite people in on our emotions.

Connecting is finding the ways that the three stories come together. The circles are overlapping in the 3Story diagram in order to communicate the connections between each story.

Doorways are entry points for the Holy Spirit to show a person his or her need for God and His ability to meet that need. Doorways often reflect a person's deepest needs, like the need for love, forgiveness, hope, security, purpose, identity, acceptance, heaven, and so forth.

Gentle Tugs are questions, observations, and reflections we use to invite our friends to connect Their Story to God's Story.

God's Story is the most important story in the universe. It includes everything in the Bible and everything He reveals to us through nature, people, and prayer.

High Points organize the crucial parts of God's Story. High points are the key parts of God's Story that a person needs to understand and trust in order to be in a growing relationship with Jesus Christ. The high points can be expressed as:

>> God loves us and created us for relationship with Him.

>> We resist relationship with God.

>> Jesus Christ lived, died, and rose to restore our relationship with God.

>> Our positive response to the Lord Jesus Christ begins our relationship with God.

Intersecting is what happens when two of the three stories come together. The intersection of the stories represents growth in the relationships: God's Story impacts My Story, My Story and Their Story come closer together, and I have the privilege of inviting my friends to respond to God's Story.

My Story is the story of who I really am and how much I really need Jesus Christ.

Overlapping is what happens when the stories come together in significant ways. The more My Story and God's Story overlap, the more I am abiding every day. The more My Story and Their Story overlap, the more I know these people and they know me. The more we know each other, the easier it is for God's Story to overlap with Their Story.

Their Story represents the story of my friends, while they are becoming more connected with My Story and ultimately more acquainted with God's Story.

Tie Points are parts of God's Story and Their Story that bring the two stories together. They are the things we share in common with the humanity of Jesus Christ; for example, feeling sad, angry, happy, being betrayed or deserted by a friend, crying, praying, being hungry, and so forth. The best way to understand tie points is to be familiar enough with the Scriptures so that the Holy Spirit can remind us of God's Story as we listen to Their Story.

VERSE MEMORIZATION INDEX

Have you ever tried to memorize lines in a play or a song? What about memorizing the answers to an upcoming test? This can be difficult, but repetition is a key to learning. Memorizing parts of God's Story is no different. You find God's Story in His Word, the Bible. Committing yourself to memorizing parts of the Bible allows God's Story to connect with your story. Memorization is one way to abide in Christ and to have His words abide in you.

On the following page you will find some key verses that illustrate part of God's Story. The first verses are foundational for understanding the 3Story life. The second section highlights key truths found in the Gospel of John. Challenge yourself to memorize parts of God's Story today. You'll be glad you did.

3STORY FOUNDATIONAL VERSES

2 Corinthians 5:14-15

For the love of Christ controls us, because we have concluded this: that one has died for all, therefore all have died; and he died for all, that those who live might no longer live for themselves but for him who for their sake died and was raised.

John 15:9

"As the Father has loved me, so have I loved you. Abide in my love."

John 15:5

"I am the vine; you are the branches. Whoever abides in me and I in him, he it is that bears much fruit, for apart from me you can do nothing."

Colossians 4:5-6

Conduct yourselves wisely toward outsiders, making the best use of the time. Let your speech always be gracious, seasoned with salt, so that you may know how you ought to answer each person.

1 Peter 3:15-16

In your hearts regard Christ the Lord as holy, always being prepared to make a defense to anyone who asks you for a reason for the hope that is in you; yet do it with gentleness and respect, having a good conscience, so that, when you are slandered, those who revile your good behavior in Christ may be put to shame.

John 1:1
In the beginning was the Word, and the Word was with God, and the Word was God.

John 3:3
Jesus answered him, "Truly, truly, I say to you, unless one is born again he cannot see the kingdom of God."

John 3:16-17
"For God so loved the world, that he gave his only Son, that whoever believes in him should not perish but have eternal life. For God did not send his Son into the world to condemn the world, but in order that the world might be saved through him."

John 8:10-11
Jesus stood up and said to her, "Woman, where are they? Has no one condemned you?" She said, "No one, Lord." And Jesus said, "Neither do I condemn you; go, and from now on sin no more."

John 14:6
Jesus said to him, "I am the way, and the truth, and the life. No one comes to the Father except through me."

John 20:30-31
Now Jesus did many other signs in the presence of the disciples, which are not written in this book; but these are written so that

you may believe that Jesus is the Christ, the Son of God, and that by believing you may have life in his name.

GETTING STARTED IN A LIFELONG RELATIONSHIP WITH JESUS CHRIST

Prayer is talking to God. Prayer is listening to God. When someone is ready to begin connecting his or her story with God's Story, the person usually starts by talking to God and listening to Him.

God invites us to pray often. He wants to hear from us and He wants to communicate with us. Many people include the following ideas when they first start to pray:

>> Explain to God how and why you need Him.

>> Thank God for loving you and creating you for the purpose of having a relationship with Him.

>> Talk to God about the way(s) you have resisted Him. (The Bible refers to this resistance as sin: going against God and His ways, rejecting His love and forgiveness, ignoring Him.)

>> Thank God for sending His Son, Jesus, to live for you, to die for your sin on the cross, and to rise from the dead for you.

>> Explain to God that you want to begin trusting Him right now.

>> Ask God to make His home in your heart.

You are off to a great start. Now make it a point to talk and listen to God every day. He longs to spend time with you. You will find prayer happening naturally the more that your story connects with His Story.